I0105707

A
PARANORMAL
LIFE

BECOMING CLAIRVOYANT

By Scott Koney

All rights reserved. No part of this book may be reproduced by any mechanical, photographic recording, nor may it be stored in a retrieval system, transmitted, or otherwise be copied for public or private use—other than "for fair use" as brief quotations embodied—without prior written permission of the author and publisher.

Copyright © 2023 Scott Koney

Printed in the United States of America
EDITOR: Stacey M. Robinson (Kya Publishing Canada)
PAGE DESIGNER: Osamudiamenabdu
COVER DESIGNER: Muhammad Kaleem
CONTRIBUTIONS: ElevatedWaves Publishing Corp.

PUBLISHER: Scott Griffin Koney (SGK) Publishing
(Avon Lake, Ohio)

ISBN (Paperback): ISBN: 979-8-9868677-0-0
ISBN (Paperback): ISBN: 979-8-9868677-1-7
ISBN (Ebook): 979-8-9868677-2-4

Library of Congress Control Number: 2022915997

CONTENT

INTRODUCTION

My whole life, I have been fascinated with the paranormal. Ever since a Wednesday in grade school when I was introduced to the show *Ghost Hunters*, I was hooked into another world that I currently can't get myself out of.

The idea of answering questions about 'what happens to us after we pass' was one that always felt somewhat obtainable through shows like *Ghost Hunters*, *Ghost Adventures*, *Celebrity Ghost Stories*, *The Haunting of...*, and *A Haunting* (to name some of my personal favorites). I have also done my fair share of reading from authors such as Margaret Doner, Zak Bagans, and books inspired and authored by demonologists Ed and Lorraine Warren.

This book is essentially the semi-chronological chain of paranormal events that have occurred since my early childhood, leading me to being the clairvoyant I am today.

The gifts I have are that I am a clairvisual and clairaudient—I can see and speak with the dead. I am also, as termed by medium Kimberly Thomas, a "super empath." I have seen ghosts, encountered extra-dimensional beings, been attacked and sexually assaulted by demons, have had visions, premonitions, and I constantly hear telepathic voices—the whole gamut of paranormal encounters.

These experiences were not only limited to me, but to other members of my family as well.

The point of this book is to tell my story as honestly as possible, at the risk of being called crazy, a fraud, or a huckster. Enclosed you will find the evidence I've gathered through photographs, screenshots, and reading from mediums.

Part One consists mostly of short stories of my experiences with the paranormal that opened me up to the reality that something strange was—and has always been—going on around me.

Part Two features my life transition into becoming a medium, and includes the reading from medium Kimberly Thomas that outlined what would essentially become my "proof" for many of the events that I experienced in *Part One*.

Part Three highlights my stories dealing with unstable/evil spirits and how it affected (and continues to affect) my everyday life. I trimmed a lot of the fat out of this book—to keep it straight to the point—and focused on the paranormal activity I have experienced, without forcing the reader to mull through a bunch of background information (that nobody wants to go through). This is all based on a true story. My story.

PART ONE:

LEADING UP TO MY GIFTS COMING TO FRUITION

EARLY CHILDHOOD EXPERIENCES

The Boy at the Pool

My childhood resembled that of many other children. Growing up the youngest of three siblings, my father worked in logistics, and my mother was a stay-at-home mom. I spent my time playing football, baseball, and basketball, and spending my summers taking swimming lessons at the Five Seasons Country Club in Westlake, Ohio with my siblings. Little did I know that the country club would become the destination of my first major encounter with an extra-dimensional being.

The Five Seasons Country Club was a fully decked-out fitness center featuring indoor racquetball courts, gyms, indoor and outdoor tennis courts, basketball courts, and a massive outdoor pool with three diving boards. This was our favorite place for my siblings and I to go on a hot summer day; there were always other children to play with, and we never had anything but a good time.

One summer day after a swim break had just finished, the lifeguards sounded the whistle to allow us to go back into the pool. I was walking to the diving boards when suddenly, I heard a voice calling for help. Next to the diving boards was an area of lawn that abutted next to one of the outdoor tennis courts. When I heard the call for help, I walked over the grass and found a hole in the ground that had never been there before—it was approximately a foot and a half in diameter—and low and behold there was a kid inside there, calmly yet persistently calling for my help.

What bewildered me was that there were other kids my age in the immediate area of this kid in the hole, no more than five feet away, but it seemed as if only I could hear and see him, as nobody else was noticing this other child's need for assistance. So naturally, I reached my arm in the hole and pulled this kid out.

The child was about my age and had dirty blond hair that was slightly curly. "Thanks!" the kid exclaimed to me. The kid and I exchanged names but for the life of me I cannot recall it, nor will I even attempt to pretend like I remember what his name was. I had so many questions about how he got stuck in a hole in the ground that was never there before, but being a young boy, I was mostly just been proud of myself for being there to be able to help the kid out. After patting myself on the back mentally, the kid and I became immediate friends.

What happened next was what truly sticks in my mind to this day. At this point we were standing by the diving boards, about twenty feet from where I "rescued" my new friend. Almost immediately after exchanging names, the kid asks me a question no young boy would say no to: "Wanna see something cool?" so of course, I said yes.

Then, with seemingly no effort whatsoever, this kid jumped in the air—and I mean *way* in the air—three times in a row. This kid had jumped what I have to guess was one hundred feet in the air, and came back down with no injury to himself nor impact on the concrete. What I noticed at this moment was that we were surrounded by other kids getting in line for the diving boards, but I was the only one experiencing what my friend was doing. No other children nor parents seemed to be seeing what I was seeing.

In a state of excitement, I go, "I have to show you to my parents!" like he was some anomaly I found (which he was). My new friend agreed, and I went to my parents sitting in lawn chairs around the pool. "Mom, Dad, this is [name forgotten]. I saved him from a hole, and he can jump one hundred feet in the air!"

Of course, being a child, my parents thought I was just exaggerating and gave me the, "Oh that's nice," but I didn't care about their impressions—I had a new friend who was basically superman. I showed my new friend around the pool as he told me this was a new place for him. After walking him around giving the grand tour of the pool, we went into the southeast corner of the pool to play with some torpedoes some other kids had left behind. But after about five minutes of playing in the water, the boy vanished into thin air.

I was so confused at this point—why did my friend ditch me? I swam around the entire pool looking for him, walked the entire perimeter of the pool and grounds surrounding it, and I even went so far as to ask random mothers in their lawn chairs if they had a child named [name forgotten], but to no avail.

At this point I was confused; had it all been a dream? No, it couldn't have been because I never woke up. My final attempt to locate my friend was to go back to the original hole that I helped him out of, in fear that he might have fallen in again. When I walked over, I discovered something even more astounding than witnessing my friend do his incredibly high vaults. What I discovered was...nothing. There was no hole, there was nothing big enough for anybody to fall in.

The only thing I came across was a small yard drain (maybe three inches in diameter) where the previous giant hole had been, certainly not something big enough for some seven-year-old boy to fall into. Little did I know that I just experienced something that opened me up to a whole extra-dimensional world.

Thoughts on the Boy at the Pool

This was one of those experiences I subconsciously suppressed in my memory, until I had a reading with medium Kimberly Thomas who brought up the incident. Writing about it today, it still doesn't feel real, but I cannot deny what I experienced.

I even went back and asked my parents, to see if they remembered me saying anything about me saving a boy at the pool, and my father said, "yes," he did.

So no, it wasn't a dream, it wasn't make-believe, and I was never one for having imaginary friends. Even as a kid, I always thought imaginary friends were *stupid*.

The full reading from Kimberly Thomas regarding this incident will be detailed, word for word, in another chapter.

Below is a screenshot from Google Earth showing the location of the pool and tennis courts, with an X marking the spot of the hole I pulled my friend out of.

Source: "Five Seasons Pool and Tennis Court." 41°28'07.74" N and 81°55'55.71" W. Google Earth. May 29, 2010. March 7, 2022.

Teleportation

Our childhood home (and still my parent's residence) is a two-story, four-bedroom house. We have a long winding staircase with a banister that goes along the entire upstairs walkway. My room is at the very end of the walkway, and is the longest walk to the top of the stairs.

When I was approximately six years old, my mom was reading to me in the rocking chair in my bedroom, a tale about Winnie the Pooh, my all-time favorite cartoon character as a young child. She was reading to me and rocking me in the chair when suddenly, I had the impulse to get up and run. I hopped off her lap and started running around the banister towards the top of the staircase. Before I reached the top of the staircase...*bam!* I'm standing on the ground floor.

I freaked the hell out. I put my hands on my head and looked around thinking, *what the heck just happened?* I stood there for moments just speechless...did I just blackout? No, I've never randomly blacked out, and still haven't to this day. What just happened? Did I just...?

I went and told my mom that I had just moved from the upstairs to the downstairs without using the staircase, but she didn't believe me. She must've thought I jumped or something like that. But I didn't. The experience left me flustered and confused for a short while.

Thoughts of Teleportation

I wish there was more to write about on this incident, but there really isn't. One second I was on the upper floor of my house and the next second I was on the ground floor. I'm truly torn on this event. Not on whether or not it happened, but whether or not I should include it in this book. I mean, who the hell would believe me when I say I teleported? Not many, unless you're familiar with ab-port, which are portals powerful entities can utilize to make something disappear from one location, and make it show up in another in the blink of an eye.

My father still doesn't believe me, and I don't blame him; it's such a fantastical concept that I don't blame him nor anyone for that matter for having their doubts regarding the incident. At that young age, teleporting wasn't even a concept I knew of yet.

This is one of those events I had to get verified through a medium (before my gifts ever came into full effect). This, too, will be further explained in another chapter where I break down the reading I had with Kimberly.

It stuck with me my entire life and I always had the question in the back of my mind, *Did I truly teleport?* I've learned through reading books regarding paranormal cases—specifically demonic infestations, where demonic (or other) powerful entities were able to dematerialize large objects such as doors and even dogs, and re-materialize them somewhere else in the house. So, why not me?

Peering Eyes and Voices in the Closet

After the teleportation incident, I never felt alone anymore. I was terrified of the dark, and could barely sleep alone in my own room. It always felt like something was watching me, just at the threshold of my bedroom door. I usually had to sleep in my brother's room on the bottom bunk or in my parent's bedroom (causing my mom to sleep in my room).

When I would sleep in my room alone, I would often wake up in the middle of the night for about an hour or so. When I would look at the threshold to my bedroom door (which I always kept open), an icy chill would run up my spine. I *knew* something was there, just outside the door. I knew something was watching me, but I couldn't see it myself.

Often I'd say, "You can come out now," but nothing would show. But in my gut, I knew there was something in that doorway peering at me. Creep.

There was one night when I was in high school and it was approximately three o'clock in the morning—also known as the witching hour—where I heard my first group of voices. For some reason I woke up in my bed, and I was laying there staring at my closet door. All of a sudden, I started to hear crying, then laughing, then crying again, then laughing again, and it continued this way. Was it coming from outside? No, this was coming from inside.

The laughing and crying got louder and louder until I realized it was coming from my closet. It got so loud that I had to leave the room and go sit in my kitchen for some peace and quiet. I sat there for about an hour until my mother came home from the night shift of the job she had recently picked up.

Startled by seeing me at the kitchen table at four A.M., she asks "What's wrong, hun?"

I replied, "There's voices coming out of my closet, Mom."

Thoughts on Peering Eyes and Voices in the Closet

I think I always had a sixth sense that I wasn't aware of until I was twenty-four years old, when my gifts truly kicked in so-to-speak. I had shamanic healing session with Dr. Robert Alcorn, a retired psychiatrist and current shamanic practitioner, and his assistant who was a light trance medium.

The medium was able to discuss what the entities were doing to me, and one of the evil entities that attached to me admitted that it attached to me at the age of seven years old because I was "an *open channel.*

After learning this, and thinking back on the experiences I had as a child, I believe I was truly sensing something watching over me and interacting with me.

The Staircase Incident

When I was a child, I was infatuated with video games (and still am to this day). One of my favorite franchises was *Metal Gear*, where you played as a special agent (with the code name Snake) and your objective was to sneak around the bad guys and progress through various missions using multiple stealth tactics.

Well, one day I decided to try and be like Snake myself. I went to the top of my staircase and climbed over the edge of the railing, and tried to hang off the edge of the stairs and climb my way down to the first floor. About halfway down, my foot slipped off the edge of the stairs and I was hanging by one hand from the banister railing. Right below me was a table with a lamp that I surely would've fell through if I let go.

As I was hanging there and slowly losing my grip, I felt this force suddenly lift me from underneath and lift me over the banister railing, with barely any effort being used on my behalf. With a rush of anxiety and astonishment, I gathered myself and wondered how in the hell did I have the strength to pull myself over the railing without breaking it? I couldn't even do a pull-up at this time in my life. Something had lifted me over the railing to prevent me from crashing into that table and lamp below me. And to that spirit, I say thank you.

Thoughts on the Staircase Incident

This, again, was another incident I had confirmed to be paranormal through a session with a medium. She actually had to bring it up for me to remember it. I remember feeling like I had superhuman strength at the moment of coming over the banister, but eventually learned that this was the help of a spirit who claimed that "that was the only way to save" me.

I actually know exactly which spirit helped me at this time, but due to personal reasons, that spirit will not be named in this book. Since coming into my gifts, she has done nothing but harass me to the point where I constantly have to wear headphones to block her out. I thank her for the times she helped me, but our relationship has turned sour. She has turned from a spirit guide to an unstable, borderline demonic, evil spirit.

Bangs on the Door

When I was seventeen years old, we had to put down one of our dogs, a yellow English lab named Gunner. Gunner had lost the use of his hind legs and had a massive tumor forming in his nasal passages that would eventually suffocate him if we did not put him down. Sadly, on February 6, 2014, we had to say goodbye to our furry family member. I was there when it happened, and I was an absolute wreck.

Dogs are my life and always have been, and all you can do at the end is just hope they know how much you loved them and what they meant to you...and I think Gunner did.

We had another dog, Tucker, who took the loss very hard. At six A.M. the next morning, he came up to my room crying and whimpering like I've never seen before. Clearly he was wondering where his best friend had gone. Unfortunately, you cannot explain to an animal that their best friend won't be around anymore, so I just had to wake up and console him until he finally fell back asleep with me in my bed.

The next day was a Friday and our high school had a day off. I was home alone with both parents at work and both siblings at college. Tucker was whimpering and refused to leave my side that day, potentially afraid another one of his friends might leave for good, too. I couldn't even go to the bathroom without this one hundred-and-ten-pound Labrador being next to me.

Well, it finally came time for me to take a shower. I stood in the bathroom, looked at Tucker, and said, "Go," pointing towards the door. He refused. Again, I said, "Go!" and he just lied down in peaceful defiance, as if it was his own way of saying no. Realizing he wasn't going to leave the bathroom for my shower, I decided to just let him stay in the bathroom with me, if it was going to make him feel better. It came to be one of the best decisions I've made, as he was a credible witness as to what happened next.

Our shower had sliding glass doors that you could easily see out of. About halfway through my shower, I decided to check on Tucker and see if he was behaving himself. I wiped the fog off of the glass door and looked out, and the second I did that, the bathroom door was banged on three times...*BANG BANG BANG!*

This happened so quickly and so aggressively that I saw the door actually bend inwards, as a result of the impacts. Tucker jumped up from his prone position and was staring intently at the door. I thought it was my dad who had come home to have a stern talking with me, so I just yelled out, "I'll be out in a minute!"

I finished up my shower, dried off, opened the door, and discovered nobody was in the house. I called both of my parents, and both were still at work. I called my grandmother (who lived about a mile away) and she said she hadn't been over to the house. I checked all the doors and they were locked, and did the same with the windows, discovering they were locked as well.

I was spooked out of my mind. Did I imagine it? No, I couldn't have because my dog Tucker reacted to it as well, so he was my credible witness in this case. Something tried to get my attention that day, and boy did it get it.

Thoughts on the Bangs on the Door

For a couple of weeks after that incident, things would be knocked off the shelves in the bathroom, which had never happened before. It seemed as if every time I entered that bathroom, a shampoo bottle would be knocked off of the shower shelf. At first, I thought this was Gunner coming back and letting us know he wasn't gone. But I know better than that now.

There's one thing the demonic does: it comes in threes. Whether it's rappings, scratches, or knocks, the demonic almost always comes in threes. They do this as an insult to the Holy Trinity, and the three bangs on the bathroom door seemed way too aggressive to be a friendly hello from the other side.

I firmly believe something was feeding off of our/my emotions of deep grief and using it to manifest itself in a time of sincere sadness. The demonic will always try to strike during the most vulnerable of times, especially during times of deep distress or when you're at your weakest, such as when you're sleeping (I've been attacked many times in my sleep, but we'll cover that in a later chapter). Nevertheless, I think this was the first time the demonic truly tried to get my attention.

The Woman in the Mirror

This incident occurred when I was twenty-three years old. I was living in a single bedroom apartment in Cincinnati where I was working for a general contractor at the time. One Saturday night my girlfriend was over, and we were drinking wine and watching game shows in my living room.

She was a tall, pretty woman with dark hair. I got up to wash my hands in the restroom while speaking to my girlfriend, who was still in the living room. As I finished washing my hands in the restroom, I saw my girlfriend in the mirror, entering into my bedroom. Assuming she was going in there to grab one of my sweatshirts, I continued talking to her and followed her into my bedroom.

But when I stepped out of the restroom, I saw that she was still sitting comfortably on the couch. I asked her, "Did you just go into my bedroom?" She replied that she had not. Flabbergasted by my experience, I sat down with her and told her, "I just saw something, and I need you to believe me. I just saw a woman enter into my bedroom and I was going to go in there because I thought it was you, but you were still sitting out here on the couch."

She replied that she believed me, but she doesn't believe in the paranormal so she essentially brushed it off. Something I could not do.

Thoughts on the Woman in the Mirror

What I saw in the mirror wasn't a doppelganger of my girlfriend at the time, but was a black-shadow woman with dark hair tied back into a ponytail. It resembled my girlfriend enough at the time to fool me into thinking it was her, but it obviously was not.

I have seen this woman since then; I sense this is a dark spirit attached to me. When trying to fall asleep in the basement of my parents' house recently, I had a flash vision of a dark-shadow woman laying exactly where I was, with sickly yellow eyes. The vision actually startled me, and I am not one who easily scares at all. She was lying exactly where I was on the couch, and I saw her from the viewpoint of the feet looking up towards the face.

The eyes were what bothered me—a wicked yellow, like somebody who was deeply jaundiced. *Was this woman in my body? Was she trying to show me that she was still with me, and does whatever I do? Was she trying to inhabit my body?*

I still have so many questions. I have never spoken to this spirit, nor do I know her name, but she seems to have been hanging around me for the past few years.

FAMILY EXPERIENCES

My Father Seeing Orbs

I wasn't the only person in my family to experience things of a paranormal nature, at a young age.

As I started coming into my abilities, I would begin to see orbs. White, golf ball-sized orbs. But not just white orbs, black orbs too. Nowadays, I mostly just see black orbs, which isn't good. As a general rule of thumb for me, seeing white orbs is good, but seeing black ones is bad, and even a potential omen of bad things to come.

One day when I was twenty-five (the age I am as I write this), after I had moved home from Cincinnati, I was eating dinner with my father at the kitchen table. We were filling our plates and I said that I had to tell him something. He gave me the go-ahead nod. I said, "Dad, I'm a medium."

And with perfect comedic timing, he looks at me and goes, "I thought you were a large." The tension was broken with laughter, and I informed my father that I could see and speak with spirits. To my surprise he countered with a story, telling me about how when he was a child he saw orbs all the time. He told me he would see white orbs flying around his bedroom, but it gradually stopped happening as he grew up. He said it was a rather common occurrence for him, but he never felt creeped out about it as nothing bad ever happened as a result of them being around.

Thoughts on My Father Seeing Orbs

For those that drew the spiritual short straw, those who are prone to paranormal activity, it is very common for this to happen at a very young age. This is when we are usually the most open and still believe in that monster under the bed. More often than not, the person will grow out of these things by the time they hit puberty—usually when they start focusing more on themselves and the "real" world around us—and they're not scared of that monster under the bed anymore. It is my belief that my dad's ability to see orbs was something that was genetically given to me, along with other gifts from family members which I will speak about next.

Great Grandmother's Sixth Sense

One thing I eventually learned from my mother is that I am not the first in the family to have the ability to see and speak with the dead. My great grandmother (on my mother's side of the family) Evelyn Mangerson had some very similar experiences prior to her passing. She had a single story cottage-style home in Bay Village, Ohio, that was only a few miles from our house ; a home that was perfect for a widowed elderly lady.

Evelyn would tell my mother how she would see things at night. She had a kitchen window that overlooked the backyard of her half acre; many times at night, she would look out and see what looked like children doing ring-around-the-rosie. This took place on many occasions, according to my great grandmother.

One day, my mother went out there to investigate for herself. What she found was a plot of flowers in the shape of the cross that seemed to resemble a grave. Was my great grandmother seeing ghostly figures dancing around a grave? We never dug up the spot to see if there was a grave underneath the flower cross—out of respect for the property and my great grandmother—but it sure was an interesting spot to see ghostly figures dancing around.

My great grandmother's experiences did not stop there. She would tell my mother that at night when she would lie down in bed to go to sleep, her deceased husband (my great grandfather Ed Mangerson) would come and lay with her and talk with her, too. She was showing no signs of dementia nor being senile at this point in her life, and she persisted to my mother that what was happening to her was real.

Thoughts on Great Grandmother's Sixth Sense

First thing that comes to my mind when I think about these events is: *is this gift something I've inherited from my great grandmother?* She seemed to be experiencing supernatural events during the psychic hours of the night (between nine P.M. and six A.M.) which is usually when supernatural activity spikes.

I was young during the time this was happening to my great grandmother, and can state for a fact that she was all there mentally, so to speak.

Other members in my family have received some gifts as well: my cousin Caroline has a photographic memory. Is it a coincidence that two of her great grandchildren have received a sixth sense of their own? It might be, but from what I've gathered, these things seem to be genetic to some degree.

Footsteps and Doors Closing

My mother and father's first house was a single story home covered with tan brick veneer on the outside, and resided across the street from Lake Erie. This home was prone to some creepy activity after the sun would fall. On many nights while laying in bed awake, my mother would hear the sound of footsteps walking up and down the hallway leading to the bedrooms. This seemed to usually only happen when my mother was awake and my father was asleep.

One night, when my mother started hearing the footsteps again, she woke up my father and asked him what it sounded like. My dad replied, "It sounds like somebody's walking in the house." Of course my dad got up to check, but nothing was there. Nothing that he could see, at least. This continued on through the duration of their time of living at this house.

That wasn't the only experience they had in that house; my parents had their first child (my oldest sibling, Jessica), and there seemed to be activity that focused around her bedroom. Every night when my mom would lay my sister down in her crib to go to sleep, she would leave the door slightly open. She would never shut it (as she wanted to be able to hear my sister should she wake up in the middle of the night and start crying). But somehow, every morning when my mother got up and went to my sister's room, the bedroom door would be completely shut.

This happened so much that my mother started testing the door out. Some nights she would leave it wide open, and in the morning it would be shut. Some nights she would leave it partially shut, and again it would be latched closed in the morning. This, combined with the footsteps, made my mother and father attribute this to something "weird" going on in the house.

Thoughts on Footsteps and Doors Closing

I believe there's always been something that's either been attached to my mom or to our family in general, because to this day, these kinds of events still happen. Hell, less than a week ago from writing this, my mother and I were sitting in the family room and we both heard the distinctive sound of somebody walking barefoot across the kitchen floor. We both locked eyes with one another, giving each other the look of, *did you hear that?*

I've been hearing footsteps in our family home all my life.

One weekend my family was in Chicago, and I literally bunkered myself in my room with my dog because our house had become rampant with footsteps coming from all over the place.

One day when my sister and I both had to leave the house for separate reasons. She was going off to graduate school, and I was going back to college. The very next morning after the day we left, my mother awoke to find both her and my bedroom doors were closed. They had been open the night before. She asked my father if he had closed the doors, and he said no. My mother called me that night to tell me about how weird it was that that had happened.

I firmly believe there is a spirit of a deceased family member that keeps a watch on all of us and is responsible for closing the doors. I believe they were closing my sister's door as a baby so she wouldn't be woken up by my parents' dog barking in the basement (or any other noise), and I believe this same spirit closed the doors to our bedrooms after it realized that my sister and I were no longer in the household anymore.

The Boy in the Window

I attended a variety of Catholic schools prior to attending college. For elementary school, I went to St. Joseph Catholic School in Avon Lake, Ohio, from first grade until the middle of seventh grade. I ended up transferring to St. Raphael's Catholic School in Bay Village because they had a better football program and more kids, which the former school was lacking. During my time at this school, I never experienced anything weird whatsoever, but one of my family members did.

We had a graduation ceremony in the school gymnasium, upon the completion of the eighth grade. The gym was packed with students and family members in attendance for our big day, but not all of the attendees came inside for the event. My mother was sitting in the bleacher section of the gymnasium and noticed during our ceremony that a boy about our age was peeking in from the upper windows of the gymnasium. She said he would walk back and forth between the second story windows, and seemed to just be watching over the class as the ceremony went on. The boy was too far away for her to see any of his features, but there was no doubt that there was a young child eying us from above.

What was strange to my mother was that when we went outside after the ceremony ended, she noted that there was no possible way for a child to get up to those windows. There was no ladder, no walkway, and no easy way to scale the roof from the ground level.

Thoughts on the Boy in the Window

I have a couple of theories about this.

Theory one: there was a boy haunting the school. There was a rumor that a boy died in the school, but I have never been able to find any concrete evidence that this actually occurred, so that theory really doesn't hold any weight to me.

Theory two: it was the boy from the pool coming to check in on me. It gives me chills just thinking about it yet it is comforting at the same time. If he was able to jump a hundred feet in the air, it wouldn't be any issue for him to jump up to the second story of a roof, right?

Regardless of who it was, this was my mother's experience and not mine. I think my mother is more "open" to these things than she realizes.

Some people are open to the paranormal and some are not. If you've made it this far and thought that these stories are bullshit—and that none of this happened, or it is all due to some undiagnosed mental illness—then you're one who is close to the paranormal. If you think that the stories are possible, or even believe one hundred percent that they happened, then you are open.

Open people are more likely to encounter the paranormal, which is why I think I've experienced so much throughout my life. Since the teleportation/dematerialization event and the pool incident, I was as open as a door with no latch. But I digress. Below is a screenshot from Google Earth showing the windows in which my mother saw the boy watching over us in the gymnasium, where you can clearly see there is no easy way to get up there without a ladder.

Source: "St. Raphael Catholic School Gymnasium." 41°28'50.31" N and 81°55'09.90" W. Google Earth. October 25, 2015. March 8, 2022.

Lead Up to Grandfather's Death

My grandfather passed away in December of 2020; this was devastating for the family, as he was the true patriarch of our family.. My grandfather had been slowly declining in the 2010s, but we were lucky enough to always have him within a mile of us. Plus, he never showed any signs of dementia or becoming senile which was tremendous because even when we had to help him out physically at times, he was still there, mentally.

He was a funny, family loving man who is currently acting as one of my spirit guides. Unfortunately, two weeks before his death, he contracted pneumonia and had a very quick decline. During those two weeks, things started happening to my parents in our household that became borderline spooky for them.

There were incidents that happened to both my mother and my father. For starters, my father was sitting in his office one afternoon working from home, when all of a sudden the paper shredder turned on by itself. This is no easy device to turn on, it had a stiff power button you had to push with some force to get it going. This happened at least two times.

Experiences seemed to happen when my dad was in his office alone. One day, it sounded like someone was being hurled down the staircase. This happened twice, and it wasn't any of the dogs as they were with him both times.

The really creepy things happened to my mom. Since my dad has sleep apnea, she would often sleep in my sister's room so she wouldn't have to listen to the sound of his breathing machine. Like me, she would always sleep with the door open, but every morning during those two weeks she would wake up and the door would be closed. It started happening enough to where she confronted my father about it and asked if he had been closing the door for her when he got up in the morning. My father replied no; the door to my sister's bedroom was already closed when he got up in the morning.

Then one night my mother was lying on the bed in my sister's room, gazing at the wall that reflected the dim night light we had in the upstairs hallway. As she was staring at the wall, she noticed the room beginning to get darker and darker until it was completely pitch black, with no light coming in except the moon light from the window. She turned around to discover that the door was closed. Something had closed the door to my sister's bedroom. She asked my father the next morning if he had come and closed the door on her and again, he said no. But what was significant about this time was that she was awake and witnessed the door close on its own.

After two weeks of my grandfather being in the hospital, he finally passed away on December 18, 2020. As soon as he passed, all the activity in the house stopped. My mom informed me about all this over the phone, while I was living in

Cincinnati, but as quickly as the activity halted at my parents' house, it escalated in my apartment.

Thoughts on the Lead Up to Grandfather's Death

I firmly believe something was trying to warn our family that something was about to happen. The activity started right before he went into the hospital and stopped (in their house, at least) the second he passed away. Whether this was deceased family members or entities of another nature behind these events happening, I'm convinced all of this was a warning that we were about to experience something tragic in the family, which we unfortunately did.

We all talked about it, and now we know that if things like that start to pick up in the house again, we have to be prepared for something to happen. It was a supernatural forewarning that my parents were not prepared for.

PART TWO:

TAKING THE INVESTIGATION INTO MY OWN HANDS

EXPERIENCES START TO BECOME PERSISTENT

Things really started to pick up when I was living alone in Cincinnati. After seeing the woman in the mirror, I realized there was something weird going on. When I would lay down in bed at night, I would constantly hear whispers and muffled conversations like somebody in the next apartment over was having a small get-together, but I never thought much of the whispers.

I would often hear footsteps coming from my apartment, but I often attributed it to the building settling. But then, the footsteps could be heard coming from inside my apartment, inside my bedroom. One night I was lying in bed, and I heard two footsteps shuffle next to my bed, and all of a sudden my television cut out. Paranormal or weird coincidence? At this point, I didn't know what to think.

One day after work I was sitting on my couch in silence, and all of a sudden I heard a few clicks. I looked around and realized that the lamp on my countertop had just turned on by itself. Curious, I walked over and turned the knob to ensure these were the clicks that I heard, and sure enough it was an exact match to the sound I had just heard.

Now, as far as the paranormal goes, I consider myself one of the bravest dudes out there. I knew something was going on in my apartment at this point, and I wasn't going to let it spook me. So naturally, I asked, "Who's in here?" A few seconds after that, the Xbox turned on by itself as I heard the three chimes (a coincidence that they turn on a device whose chimes come in threes, just like the demonic?).

So, after confirming I was not alone, I went and sat back down on the couch, and began scrolling through my phone. This type of thing did not phase me. No more than ten minutes after I sat back on the couch, I noticed a bright light flashed next to me causing me to jump back and look around trying to figure out where it came from. Then I noticed it—the overhead light in my kitchen had turned on by itself. After I came into my gifts, I learned that this was my recently deceased grandfather trying to get my attention. I knew he found it funny to watch me try to solve the puzzle. But still, at this point, I wasn't afraid.

My Xbox would always turn on by itself. I tried to debunk it, because it has a sensor you barely need to touch to turn it on. I would blow on it to see if the air conditioning was turning it on, I would hold my finger slightly in front of it, I would even say, "Xbox, power on," but nothing would work.

This would prove to be a significant event in the near future when my friend Sean came over.

Sean was and still is one of my best friends. We were roommates in college and met when I joined the fraternity Beta Theta Pi. Him and I were party animals when we were at the

University of Dayton, and we were lucky enough to live within thirty minutes of one another after graduation.

About once or twice a month, Sean would come over; we'd drink and smoke and listen to music while telling stories. Well one day I started telling Sean about what was happening in my apartment—hearing the muffled whispers, the footsteps, the woman in the mirror, and the lights turning on by themselves. I was finishing a tirade about all that has been happening in the apartment and I ended it with "…and that's why I'm so curious about the Xbox always turning on by itself!" and at that very second, we heard the three chimes of the Xbox (that was no more than three feet away from us) turning on.

The look on Sean's face was priceless. I saw somebody become a bona fide believer for the first time. I literally grabbed his hand and looked him in the eye while he tried to gather himself and told him, "This is real." I think something was listening in on our conversation and was trying to prove to Sean that yep, something *is* here, and *here I am.*

TAKING THE INVESTIGATION
INTO MY OWN HANDS

After the incident with Sean, I was hellbent on getting answers. *What was in my apartment and what did it want with me?* I tried making my own Ouija board, which is one of the dumbest things I've ever done in my entire life. Even though I didn't receive any communication, Ouija boards can still open portals and bring demonic entities into your life that are not easy to get rid of (to say the least).

I tossed the board in the trash after a quick realization of how things could've turned ugly, quickly. I then found this app on my iPhone, one that would allow you to communicate with spirits. The app had a built-in dictionary and would allow spirits to give you one word responses based on changes in the environment that were measured using the phone's innumerable sensors. The app would also give a direct reading of EMF (electromagnetic frequency) which is a strong indicator of a spirit's presence. It works similar to the ovilus devices you see on shows like *Ghost Adventures*.

The way the app worked: you would open it on your phone, ask a question, and just wait for a response. The responses would save in an internal database, and then you could export them to your Notes app. Often, it would spit out random words that didn't mean anything.

At first, I thought it was a joke—there was no way it could actually work! But then I started getting direct responses to questions; mostly, I started getting predictions about what would happen in my future. I used the application on and off for about two months while I was sitting in my apartment bored because it was entertaining for me. Unfortunately, I think I unknowingly opened a portal for spirits because when you open yourself up for communication from the spirit world, all types of things can come through. Both the good and the bad.

My first day using the application (which I will not name because I discourage anybody from using it due to the harm it potentially poses) was February 15, 2021, and some of the first words that came out were predictions that would come to fruition in the near future.

2/15/2021 - 8:18 PM: SET (.46)
2/15/2021 - 8:21 PM: BURNING SKIN (.46)
2/15/2021 - 8:22 PM: ROCKS (.7)

My first set of future predictions was "BURNING SKIN" and "ROCKS." At the time, I thought these were just random words being spat out by the device. Little did I know, these would hold significant value due to the harm they would bring me and almost to my dog, Nina.

On August 6, 2021, I experienced my first attack by a malevolent entity. I was sitting on my couch when suddenly I started experiencing a searing burn on my back left shoulder blade. By this time, I had come into my gifts of being able to hear and see spirits, which happened in June of 2021.

As soon as I felt the scorching burn start to happen, I heard a spirit telling me, "I'm sorry! I'm sorry!" This was from a spirit that had failed to protect me from an attack against something evil.

Below is the photo where you can see the faint red marks on my back and shoulder blade (please excuse the dirty mirror). The marks on my back only lasted for a maximum of five minutes before they disappeared completely, so I'm glad I was able to get photographic evidence in time. This made me truly start to question the nature of what I was dealing with.

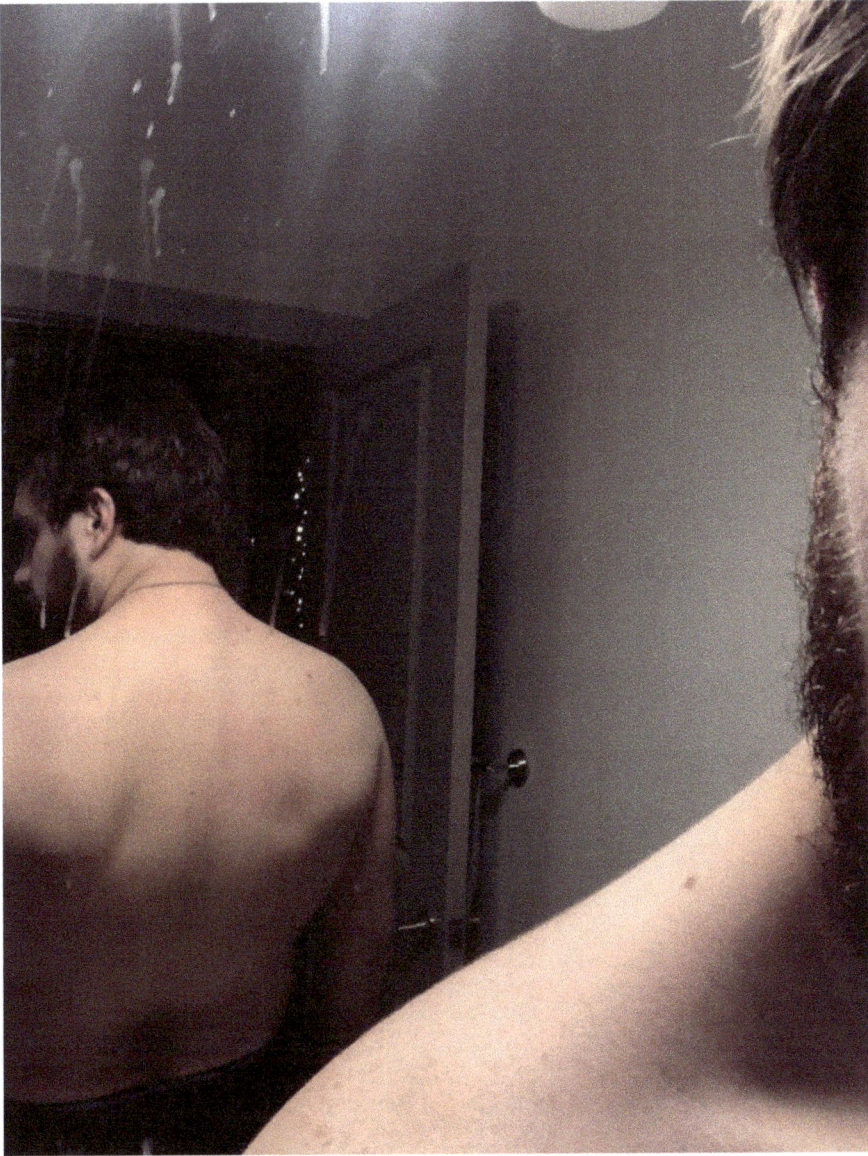

The second prediction from the first set of words was "ROCKS." Around the same time as the burn, something unexplainable had happened in my apartment. I had come home from work one day and greeted my black English lab, Nina, who I had recently adopted. After taking her outside to go on a walk, I come back in to find a pile of black rocks neatly stacked in the middle of the floor of my apartment. This puzzled me because I couldn't explain this for the life of me. These couldn't have been brought inside by her because I always kept an eye on her and she never once tried to grab a rock, let alone hold a mouthful of them along a walk and up three flights of stairs to my apartment. The windows and patio door were closed so no critter could've gotten in and brought these along with them. I thought of every explanation until I finally learned about ab-ports.

An ab-port is when a particularly powerful entity is able to transfer items from one location to another by de-materializing them in the location of origin and re-materializing them in their desired location. There was a specific guide of mine (who wishes to remain unnamed in this book), who told me there was an entity that liked to hang out in my bedroom, and was trying to suck the life force out of my dog.

To the best of my knowledge, I believe this entity ab-ported these rocks into my apartment while I was at work to try and get my dog to eat them to hurt her, or worse. Below is a photo of the rocks after I picked them up and placed them on the windowsill.

Sidenote: As I was writing this, I felt something hit the top of my shoe and bounce into the wall of my desk under me. It felt and sounded exactly like a small rock, but I can't find any rocks nor anything else that could've hit me. Strange, huh?

Now this leads us to our third prediction: "CELLS" and "HEALER."

2/15/2021 - 8:59 PM: BRING HER (1)
2/15/2021 - 8:59 PM: PLACE (.52)
2/15/2021 - 8:59 PM: START (.54)
2/15/2021 - 9:00 PM: CELLS (.47)
2/15/2021 - 9:01 PM: HEALER (.45)

When I had my first reading with medium Kimberly Thomas, she told me that I had the ability to heal and "shift the cells of others" just by touching them. She told me that I had the gifts of healing. *Again, this will all be outlined in the next chapter when I detail my thirty minute reading with Kimberly.*

Now to "DONT BLINK."

```
2/15/2021 - 9:43 PM: BREAK FREE (.52)
2/15/2021 - 9:43 PM: DONT BLINK (.69)
2/15/2021 - 9:44 PM: WEIGHT (.51)
```

This event brought me joy like a kid on Christmas. I was sitting in my chair playing music and watching the app spew out its words. Then all of a sudden, the words "DONT BLINK" came across the screen. As soon as they did, I looked up, and a massive orb flew right at my face and then quickly changed directions and narrowly avoided my head, going right over it.

Something was legitimately interacting with me at this point, and I loved it. I actually remember laughing and clapping at how great of an experience it was, because for a novice paranormal investigator, this was like the Holy Grail. Getting evidence on both my phone and in person was an experience I truly cherished at the time.

When we were kids, my friends and I used to mess with each other and play the flinch game. We'd pretend we were going to hit the other person, and if they flinched then we gave them "two for flinching," which means you punched them in the arm twice. It was a game about seeing who the manliest guy was. That's exactly the game that was being played with me, and I didn't flinch.

Now to "WARN HARSH ROADWAY DEVELOPER STAY AWAY."

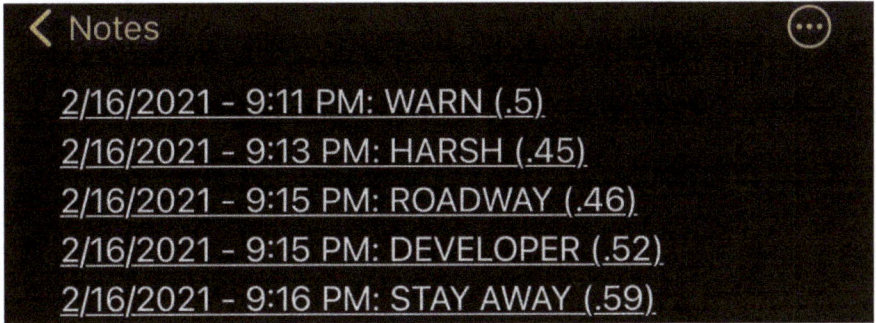

Notes

2/16/2021 - 9:11 PM: WARN (.5)
2/16/2021 - 9:13 PM: HARSH (.45)
2/16/2021 - 9:15 PM: ROADWAY (.46)
2/16/2021 - 9:15 PM: DEVELOPER (.52)
2/16/2021 - 9:16 PM: STAY AWAY (.59)

This next prediction was borderline creepy. The words "WARN HARSH ROADWAY DEVELOPER STAY AWAY" were a true warning. The spirit was either looking out for me, or proving to me that it could predict the future, because two days after I got these words I popped a tire in a manhole-sized pothole just on the outskirts of my apartment complex. Either way, the spirit was right. I put a bullet hole-sized puncture in my front right tire. Picture of the tire is below to prove it.

Now, one of my favorite interactions I've had with a spirit through the app.

```
2/22/2021 - 8:22 PM: SOFIA (.68)
2/22/2021 - 8:26 PM: WALL (.51)
2/22/2021 - 8:27 PM: RUMOR (.64)
2/22/2021 - 8:27 PM: HUNG (.47)
2/22/2021 - 8:29 PM: BEGIN (.49)
2/22/2021 - 8:29 PM: STOP MOVING (.49)
2/22/2021 - 8:30 PM: LENGTH (.5)
2/22/2021 - 8:31 PM: FLASH (.55)
2/22/2021 - 8:31 PM: BUSH (.52)
```

Now this message wasn't a prediction, but it was certainly promiscuous. Some spirit named Sofia was telling me that there was a "rumor" that I was "hung" and wanted me to "begin" to "flash" my "bush." This made me laugh at the time...and still does (although it creeps me out a bit, knowing she could be watching me when I get undressed). Either way, thanks for the laugh, Sofia.

3/9/2021 - 8:21 PM: RANGE (.47)
3/9/2021 - 8:21 PM: MUSIC (.53)
3/9/2021 - 8:22 PM: NOMINEE (.46)
3/9/2021 - 8:22 PM: OUTSTANDING (.45)

I don't know what spirit was saying the words "RANGE MUSIC NOMINEE OUTSTANDING," but they sure were flattering to me.

At the time I had been living alone in my apartment for over a year, and had spent much of my free time singing along to my music. I have a whole playlist of songs I can sing somewhat decently to. The walls in my apartment were acoustically insulated very well, so I never felt nervous about bothering neighbors, and the acoustics of the apartment weren't bad at all.

I was actively singing along to "One Man Can Change the World" by Big Sean, Kanye West, and John Legend, and these words started to appear on the screen. I'm no opera singer, but I learned how to hit and hold more than a few notes in my time living alone. The girlfriend (that I had previously mentioned in this book) had broken up with me over an argument we had, but she was a music teacher at an elementary school who had the voice of an angel. She had heard me sing and told me that I was actually "pitch perfect," which I didn't even know what that meant at the time. But nonetheless, I was complimented by a spirit and I excitedly said, "Thank you!" out loud.

It was a good feeling to be complimented, but also a little weird to learn that I had an audience that I couldn't see.

3/24/2021 - 8:30 PM: AMONG (.45)
3/24/2021 - 8:32 PM: ANGEL (.47)
3/24/2021 - 8:34 PM: BRIELLE (.45)
3/24/2021 - 8:36 PM: CONCERN (.47)
3/24/2021 - 8:38 PM: TEND (.48)
3/24/2021 - 8:41 PM: BLIND (.45)
3/24/2021 - 8:42 PM: DECLINE (.76)
3/24/2021 - 8:42 PM: MONEY (.54)
3/24/2021 - 8:43 PM: OUT (.46)
3/24/2021 - 8:44 PM: COSTLY (.57)
3/24/2021 - 8:44 PM: DEATH (.49)
3/24/2021 - 8:44 PM: SUSPICION (.47)

This grouping of words was very special to me. It seems as if an actual angel was talking to me. I don't know if her name is Brielle, but I've come to learn that the name Brielle means God is [my] strength. To me, this was a message from a higher power that was telling me to "tend" to the "blind" (those who can't see spirits?) and to "decline money" for my services.

I didn't know exactly what she wanted me to do, but it seemed like she wanted me to do something very important. The last word "SUSPICION" was what really struck me. I encountered spirits that wanted to mess with me, show them my privates, and I was very suspicious of the words that were coming across the screen at that time, not sure if they were from a real angel, and she called me out for it!

```
3/24/2021 - 11:01 PM: FOCUS (.48)
3/24/2021 - 11:02 PM: MEDIUM (.5)
3/24/2021 - 11:03 PM: INTEGRITY (.47)
3/24/2021 - 11:04 PM: INHERIT (.63)
3/24/2021 - 11:04 PM: REFUGE (.48)
3/24/2021 - 11:10 PM: PILL (.49)
3/24/2021 - 11:11 PM: RAISE (.47)
```

It took me a long time to learn what these words meant. I was already coming into my gifts of being a medium/clairvoyant, but I hadn't realized it until the month of June. The spirits wanted me to "focus" and get into a meditative state to use my gifts of being a "medium."

The "PILL RAISE" refers to the medication I was taking at the time, Adderall, which I would come to learn was raising my abilities of being a medium. That will be covered in a future chapter where my deceased grandfather and I had a heated conversation.

Now, onto some helpful advice from my grandfather.

```
3/25/2021 - 2:00 AM: GRANDFATHER (.48)
3/25/2021 - 2:00 AM: PHYSICIAN (.78)
3/25/2021 - 2:00 AM: SUBJECT (.58)
3/25/2021 - 2:00 AM: WORM (.81)
3/25/2021 - 2:00 AM: REPORT (.54)
3/25/2021 - 2:01 AM: US (.47)
3/25/2021 - 2:03 AM: NOAH (.45)
3/25/2021 - 2:04 AM: ANIMAL (.46)
3/25/2021 - 2:05 AM: INTERIOR (.58)
3/25/2021 - 2:06 AM: STOOL (.45)
```

This was another spooky prediction. This was my grandfather "reporting" to me that my dog, Nina, which came out as "Noah," had contracted worms. Due to this grouping of words, I actually made an appointment with the veterinarian for the next week and discovered that my dog did in fact contract worms. Thanks, Grandpa.

```
4/6/2021 - 6:29 PM: JUNE (.49)
4/6/2021 - 6:29 PM: EMILY (.51)
4/6/2021 - 6:30 PM: TELEPATHY (.51)
4/6/2021 - 6:33 PM: LESSER (.45)
4/6/2021 - 6:34 PM: EXTERNAL (.58)
4/6/2021 - 6:34 PM: SALLY (.46)
4/6/2021 - 6:35 PM: FOR ME (.52)
4/6/2021 - 6:36 PM: MORE (.69)
4/6/2021 - 6:36 PM: LUCAS (.46)
4/6/2021 - 6:38 PM: IMPLY (.47)
4/6/2021 - 6:41 PM: REAP (.53)
4/6/2021 - 6:42 PM: MOTHER (.75)
4/6/2021 - 6:42 PM: PREPARE (.66)
4/6/2021 - 6:43 PM: PROVIDER (.48)
4/6/2021 - 6:44 PM: GOODBYE (.55)
4/6/2021 - 6:44 PM: UNIVERSE (.49)
```

This line of answers from the app had two distinct messages in it; one was a prediction, and the other was a malevolent entity messing with me.

Let's start with the first three words: "JUNE EMILY TELEPATHY." Anybody want to guess when my telepathy started? In June. In June of 2021, I had my first telepathic experience with my grandfather, but I will cover that in a later chapter. I had come to learn through another guide that Emily was one of our deceased family members who is actually my mother's spirit guide, and she was warning me that my gifts were going to kick in in June.

Now for the next message: "REAP MOTHER PREPARE PROVIDER GOODBYE UNIVERSE." There is a specific entity, a djinn, who has a lot of power and likes to mess with me. Once I came into my abilities in June, he told me that my mother was going to pass away. I was concerned enough to call her and tell her to just keep her stress low and to be careful in general. So that being said, this was the djinn messing with me trying to get me worked up thinking my mother was going to die. Djinn can often be tricksters, and I am happy to report that my mother is still alive and in good health.

READING FROM
MEDIUM KIMBERLY THOMAS

After months of using the communication app on my phone, I had more questions than answers and I decided to consult a professional. I looked up multiple mediums and found Kimberly Thomas' website and decided to book an appointment for a Saturday morning. After starting the session with a short prayer, I started asking her the questions that were on my mind, but kept it very vague in the beginning to see what she could pick up on.

Below is a verbatim conversation I had with her.

Kim: So Scott, tell me about what you're after—what's on your mind?

Me: So essentially, I've been experiencing things my entire life—somewhat of a paranormal nature, and as of lately, things would be picking up when something bad was happening. Like, you'll have what I'll just call an influx of activity two weeks before my grandfather died, and as soon as he passes all the activity stopped. I'm experiencing things like that, and it's not just me, my family is experiencing things like that. And now, more specifically the past few months, I've either increased my ability to notice these things, or they've decided to become more present around me, and I want to know which one it is.

Kim: I am going to say that while you were just starting to describe what's going on in your life (or what has happened in your life), the atmosphere around you is highly, highly charged, and I want to say you are part of that high level of energy that is going on around you, in particular. The way the spirit actually presents it [to me] is like lightning bolts, and that's just for me to say there's a lot of energy around you and that you are, like discharging energy off of yourself as well. I think you take it in. I'll call you like the super empath; you're like a lightning rod. And I am talking about you personally, maybe we'll get to other family members in a moment here, but you do have this energy right now about you. And you are also, what I'm hearing is, you are not afraid of your emotions, right? Would you say that's true?

Me: Correct.

Kim: Yeah, you're not afraid of them at all. You don't, you know you want to have appropriate emotions in certain situations, but you are very much aware that when you're feeling happy you're happy, when you're feeling sad, you're sad, and you claim it. You don't try to brush it away, and this is powerful about you.

There was something that happened to you at a very early age. And I'm just going to say spirit is showing a picture of you around four years old. I feel like what I'm seeing is a four-year-old. There was something significant that happened to you at an early age, and if you say, "No I was five, or six," that's OK, but there was something that happened to you at that age that kind of triggered this openness to the magic of the world. The openness to the metaphysical part of the world, OK? And they have you in an outdoor situation right now; I don't see the people that are around you right now, but there was something that happened to you when you were a lot younger, and you've been like really, really, really, really open ever since.

Me: Was it by a pool maybe? Was it by a pool?

Kim: Oh gosh, OK, thank you for that. I felt like water was near by, but I couldn't tell if it was natural or not. Water is nearby in this image that they're giving me. So, what happened?

Me: What I'm thinking of, I might not be right, but what I'm immediately thinking of is there used to be this pool our family would go to at this country club, and I had what I thought was this dream that I pulled some other young kid out of a well, like right next to where the pool was. And then, I was hanging out with this kid, and I couldn't tell if I woke up or whatever happened, and then I looked back and there was this small three inch pipe there like there's no way a kid could fit in there and I was hanging out with this kid for a while. Now maybe that's what it was?

Kim: OK.

Me: I could be wrong.

Kim: OK. But this is good because what I said triggered a memory within you; this is a good thing. So, I'm going to say that's probably when you became even more open. As a matter of fact, who is this little...boy? [Kim goes silent]. So, this little boy that you feel like you pulled out of a well?

Me: Yeah, it was like a well or a big pipe—like a manhole, almost.

Kim: I feel like that entity—I'm going to switch to the word entity—I don't feel like it was like a human boy, per se; I'm going to say entity. And, because spirit keeps changing the picture of this boy in my mind's eye from just being a boy, to a boy with wings, to a boy that can do supernatural type things like leap up high in the air and come back down without injury and that kind of thing. So, I'm just going to say that you did have some kind of, I'm going to say good, good energy/entity experience at this age. This is all good. Now you felt like you were helping this person, right? You felt like you were doing your job; you didn't hesitate right?

Me: No.

Kim: Yeah, this was all good. This is very, very, very good, even though I feel like this boy was more...I want to say angel, but spirit is saying no, not quite...not quite an angel; not quite. It was an entity, but a different type of entity that's on the good side, that has positive energy. Maybe this is one of your guides (or something like that) that just showed himself to you at a very, very early age through this event.

But let's get back to the present moment; you've got all this energy which is really actually impacting your physical environment around you, and I want to say it's your fault. [laughs]

Me: For feeding it?

Kim: Yeah. [continues laughing]

Me: For giving it all the attention I have?

Kim: Yes.

Me: I know what I did. I got a little device on my phone that would give me one-word answers, because I couldn't tell if I was experiencing things around me or if my mind is playing tricks on me, so I got this device that would give one word responses and I was able to start kinda gauging when something is around me.

Kim: OK, but you really don't need that device. You really don't need that device to let you know when spirits are around. It just kind of confirms it for you.

Me: Mhm, correct. It's just what I was doing when I was first getting into it.

Kim: OK, OK, so you are attracting. What I would say to you is, are you working withon purpose, working with your guides, or angels?

Me: Yes.

Kim: OK, and are you letting them know how you want these experiences to unfold in your life, or are you still just at the mercy of these experiences?

Me: I'm not so at the mercy, but I've asked, like I have a dog and my dog would get very unnerved when something's around, and I would just ask them, "Please, if you could give her a break, she's getting anxious?" and things would calm down. And then I'd just say thank you. That's kind of how I interact.

Kim: OK, OK, that's very good. So, I am going to go quiet and I'm going to ask on your behalf, who is really there with you most of the time, and who hopes you manifest the kind of reaction you want in those moments. I don't feel like you're alone. I do feel like you have a guide with a lot of power. A lot of real power that this guide manifests physically around you. I keep getting the word "shaman." Have you ever studied shamanism at all? I feel like you've got a guide that is a shaman.

Me: I'm not super familiar with it, but I don't look at it as being unrealistic.

Kim: So this particular shaman...I'm hesitating because I want to describe him to you, and I want to do my typical medium thing, but I want the shaman to really present himself in a way that you can relate to, and not me. This shaman, if he were to manifest himself, he appears to me as a very old man.

Me: Yes, I've seen an old man with a small white goatee (which I had seen in pictures I had captured).

Kim: And he's on the thin side, so if he were human [is he not human?], you would equate him with the way Ghandi barely ate in the last years of his life. Would you agree with that or not? I see a very thin man.

Me: I've only ever pictured a face, or seen a face in a photo.

A Paranormal Life: Becoming Clairvoyant

Kim: OK, so, I'm just going to tell you that, he doesn't want me to call him Native American, but if I had to represent him in some kind of way, I would say that he's Asian and Indian.

Me: Some of the words I got on my device would be Indian and Japanese.

Kim: OK, it's kind of like a mix for me. So, I feel like it's the shaman, and this shaman entity [notice how she did not say human] knew you...has known you for multiple lives. And this is the life that he wants you to be brave and be as magical and as mystical as Merlin. You know those characters that we read about that can wave a wand and they can make magic happen? The alchemist, and those kinds of folks, the magicians? You have the ability; you have a greater ability to actually...you're a nature wizard.

You can impact the environment around you, and that's what you do. You could go outside if you really wanted to practice harnessing the wind, to have the wind blow around you, you could do that if you want to do that. That's within your purview in this lifetime to manifest, if you want to do that.

Having said that, what the shaman is all about though is to use your gifts in order to heal those around you. And I'm going to go as far as to say, when I'm talking about healing, I'm not just talking about work like I'm doing being a medium and helping people through their grief, but I'm talking about physical healing.

I don't know; this is such a different type of reading for me. The shaman is saying you could shift the cells/energy level of others if you wanted to pursue that type of physical healing. Having said that, we have to be careful because let's say you do pursue that, Scott. Let's say you do have this ability—through your training or mentoring, or however you go about doing that—you do have success at seemingly helping people get physically better, keep in mind that the people that submit to your healing beliefs, your healing outflow of energy, they have to be receptive. They have to welcome and want that in their lives. So, you have to understand that even though I'm talking to you in terms of being like Merlin and being able to affect things around you, this is a cooperative and collaborative universe. So, when you embark upon this journey, the people that you can help and that you can impact their lives, those are the people that will be drawn to you.

You don't have to pursue anything. You wouldn't have to put up a shingle and say, "I'm here," and maybe do some marketing and try and get some people to come to you. This is one of those organic things about you. So I've gone off the deep end too much on this shamanism with you, but that's everything that's coming through. So this shaman will help you understand what you need to do to have the kind of atmosphere in your surroundings on the basis that you want.

I mean, if you don't ever want to have to say, "Leave my dog alone," again, this shaman is here to help you conjure up, if you will, the energy within your environment that kinda keeps, or dampens the strength of the other spirits that are around you. They'll always be around, but we can't, like, dampen their effects or their impacts on others around us. I will say to you, personally, don't ask to ever shut off your gifts or anything like that [which I have done countless times]. What you want *to know about yourself is how does this work, and how can I get it to work in my favor in a more positive way that is not only good for me but is good for the people and the animals and those around you—that's what you want.*

You never really want to shut down yourself. I would say meditation is going to be key. I really feel that if you get into meditations, that the shamans that are physically here on earth use, I think they would do you a world of good, because that would connect you even more greatly with the shaman that is your guide.

There are people that they just know that they're earth shamans; it's just within them. It's, you're a male, I'm female, and they would say I'm a shaman. It wouldn't be about going to school and finding out you're a shaman; some people just know that's who they are. If I were in your shoes, that's the kind of shaman that I would seek out: someone that knew it growing up, and then they embraced it, and now they are practicing shamanism.

Me: Uhhhhh...OK. May I ask...what the next step would be to develop in my greatest potential?

Kim: From a spiritual gift standpoint, is that what you're talking about?

Me: Yes.

Kim: OK. [Kim goes silent] There are, for you, they're showing me different images here. You are really meant to study anything of a mystical nature that deals with nature—that deals with being out in nature. You know there are pagan beliefs that deal with loving the earth, and the nature elementals that exist. You've heard about fairies and things like that; I'm just going to tell you that those things actually do exist, that there are spirits that are born of the earth, OK? And, I'm just going to right in this moment, become more curious about spirits of nature, and how when you're out in nature, and...I keep hearing drum beats in the background in my head.

I know there's something about the shamanic journey with a drum beat behind it, so I'm just going to say you really need to start reading about shamanism and being drawn to a path. I'm just going to say, don't be afraid of paganism that deals with things of nature. Your long-term journey—if you want to continue to communicate with spirits and that kind of thing—that's all part of it, but the bigger part of your journey really is about healing others.

Healing others is going to be the ultimate [goal]. And this is a long-term journey; this is nothing that in the next ten years you're going to say, "I've arrived." It's not like that. It's always going to be learning more and more and more, but it's going to start with studying mother earth and nature and that shaman side.

Me: OK. I will say that I have one last question—kind of a big one. This reading reminded me, around the same time, about four years old around the same time as the other incident, actually maybe a little younge. I was in my bedroom and was sitting in my mom's lap and she was reading me a story. I got up and started walking towards the stairs, and all of a sudden, *like I teleported*, I was on the ground floor. I was like, "What just happened?" My mom didn't believe me, and I thought maybe I just zoned out. I don't know what happened; is there anything to that?

Kim: You know, that's really interesting that you would say that because this whole reading for you from my viewpoint has been one about magic. About really [Kim laughs] different viewpoints on life. I mean this is a rare, rare sharing experience that I'm having here. I have to say it, Scott, you're special! [Kim continues laughing] You're very special.

Me: I hope it's a good experience!

Kim: So this teleporting thing: first of all, I believe you. As a matter of fact, I've got goosebumps from your story that you just told, and when I get goosebumps, that means that's true, this is real, this is not something fake. So when you were four years old, I'm picking up a person that had already passed away that you are related to, it was either a grandmother or a great grandmother. This is a woman that comes through, and she passed away, and for some reason they're saying the nineteen-thirties to me. I don't know if that means anything to you. I don't know if that's when she passed away.

Me: I had a vision two nights ago of a tall elderly lady and I was sitting next to her in a hotel lobby, and she was dressed very old-timey. [During this vision, it was in the early 1900s and she was saying something to me that I couldn't understand]. So it might be her?

Kim: So, she's telling me in this moment, I feel like this is great grandmother, again, I feel like we are connecting to truth here. And she says to me, "I had to save him in that moment, and that was the only way to save him." She actually kind of like scooped you up and grabbed you and had you land safely. You had a great chance of being hurt or falling or doing something, and she kind of, like, decided it ain't happening today. OK? And she saved you.

Me: Oh, I remember I was hanging off the stairs at some point. Huh, wow, yeah, I know what she's talking about.

Kim: OK. So, you've just had a blessed supernatural life from the get-go, and it's wonderful from my viewpoint; it might not be wonderful from your viewpoint.

Me: It is wonderful; I am blessed.

Kim: OK. To acknowledge all of this stuff is just great. So, your great grandmother—that's why you teleported, and yes you did teleport, and it doesn't matter if nobody else believes you. Don't sweat that. It happened, and now you know why.

Me: Oh my God.

Kim: OK. So you know, Scott, I don't know how you're doing financially. But this spirit wants you to know don't worry about that; your pockets are going to get fat in the future—fat with gold. Which means you're going to be much more financially well-off than what you're thinking about now, OK? So don't worry about that; I have to tell you that, since it's given to me.

Me: That's...incredible to know, wow.

Kim: Well, I'm glad you called, and I just feel blessed to have been the one to help you get some insights to what's going on with you, so thank you for reaching out to me—this was good for me, too.

PART THREE:

COMING INTO THE GIFTS

FIRST CONTACT

So by now, I had my reading with Kimberly Thomas and was blown away by what she told me. Am I really a nature wizard? Do I really have the capability to harness the wind? Am I meant to be a shaman? I had so much to ponder about.

For the next few days, I would spend my free time re-listening to the reading through the audio file she sent me via Dropbox, but at least now I had answers about what was happening in my apartment. I wasn't crazy. There truly were entities around me that I was interacting with and that were trying to get my attention. Little did I know, my abilities were about to kick in like a motherfucker.

I was working as an estimator and pre-construction engineer for a general contractor in Cincinnati, and I was working on a bid package with my boss when I started hearing whispers. I would hear, "I hate this kid," when I didn't have my headphones in. I would start to look around and wonder who said that to me.

I was very self-conscious about how my boss viewed me, and I was wondering if he was saying it under his breath, but I would turn around and ask if he said anything and he said, "no." This kept happening to the point where I was convinced one of my coworkers was talking about me. It was like I was hearing someone from across the room talk about me. I knew it was about me, but I couldn't tell where it was coming from.

I began to ignore it, figuring somebody was just having problems with somebody else, or if they had a problem with me it would be brought up to me directly. Little did I know, these were words being communicated to me telepathically by an unseen entity—the shaman.

A big part of my job was making phone calls to subcontractors to see if they would bid on jobs for us. I would often spend three to four hours on the phone throughout a day in a separate huddle room just pounding the phone. One day shortly after my reading with Kimberly, I was sitting back making a phone call and listening to the phone ring, when all of a sudden the television remote in front of me started spinning. I didn't think anything of it. Maybe I just bumped the table and caused it to spin a bit. No big deal. Then later that night, I'm sitting on my couch watching some television on my home theater projector, and suddenly the bag of almonds I had on the coffee table started spinning in the same way in front of me. I didn't bump the table, nor was this an object that was prone to be able to move easily as it was a big three-pound bag. I quickly made the correlation to the remote spinning in front of me earlier that day and realized that something was trying to get my attention. This didn't bother me, so I brushed it off and ignored it for the time being.

A couple of nights after that, I came face to face with my first entity (well, technically, second if you count the DONT BLINK experience). I was sitting on the right-hand side of my couch, and was leaning forward, watching television once again. I then decided to grab my phone which was sitting on the arm rest. I lifted my right arm to grab the phone and was shocked to find that there was a golf ball sized pure white orb sitting on top of my phone. I quickly shifted in my seat and adjusted my point of view to make sure this wasn't some glare from the kitchen light being reflected off of the phone screen. Well, it sure wasn't a glare!

The orb slowly-but-surely proceeded to float up in front of my face, so close that I could reach out and grab it. It got eye-level with me and stopped. The orb and I stared at each other for a couple of seconds before it slowly started moving towards my face, and when it was mere inches away, vanished right before my eyes. This was a calm-yet-exciting experience.

There was something peaceful about the orb. It wasn't moving erratically, nor did it feel threatening. It came off to me as something that was just hanging out and watching the projector with me, and when I noticed it, the entity just decided to show itself to me. I didn't get frightened in the least. It almost felt angelic in a way. Whatever it was, I didn't think it was a malevolent entity.

FIRST TELEPATHIC CONVERSATION

Once again, I was sitting on the couch in the living room of my apartment. At this time, I had a huge weed problem. Every second of the day I spent outside of work I would be high. I would come home from work and immediately just start taking rips off of my bong. It was medicine to me; I even have the medicinal card, so it was technically legal for me to do so. What I didn't know was that when I would smoke weed, the effects would make me able to see spirits more clearly than when I was (rarely) sober.

Well, one day I was smoking in silence and I started spacing out and staring at things around my apartment when I looked over to the kitchen. I noticed what seemed like a figure made out of transparent, static, almost like heat waves coming off of an asphalt road on a scorching summer day.

As I stared at this figure, wondering if I was just too high, the figure floated over the counter, got right in my face and loudly asked me, "How you doing today?" There was no mistaking it: this was my grandfather voice, John Biesterfeldt, and it came with his classic phrase that he would start every conversation with. Every time I would call him, he would answer with a cheerful, "How you doing today?"

I immediately broke down into tears because he had passed about six months prior, but I knew this was his voice. I cried and gathered myself and asked out loud, "Grandpa?"

I heard a faint, "Yup," and sat in the eerie silence wondering if I was having a mental break. I started thinking to myself, *what the hell was going on?*, but when I was thinking I noticed I could literally *hear* myself thinking. Imagine hearing your own voice echoing on a megaphone from far away. That's exactly what it sounded like. It's like hearing yourself talk in a distant room of the house you're in. For the first time, I was hearing myself telepathically communicate. I was coming into my clairvisual and clairaudient abilities at the same time. Filled with anxiety and fear, I grabbed both my dog and my headphones and took her out of the apartment to go on a two-mile walk to get my head straight.

It was about midnight, and I was walking by some train tracks when I decided to take my headphones out and see if I was still hearing my grandfather's voice.

I ask in my head, "Grandpa?"

Sure enough, I hear him say, "I'm here, and so is Uncle Dennis." Dennis Koney was from my dad's side of the family and had passed about five years prior, due to heart failure. I only met him a handful of times before his passing, but without trying to sound too mushy he made a tremendous impact on my heart and quickly asserted himself to be one of my favorite people in our extended family.

I ask both my uncle Dennis and my grandfather John, "What are you doing here?" The reply was spine-chilling.

"We're here to break you in...to telepathy." I quickly froze up with fear.

"Wait, so I'm a medium?" I asked.

"Uh-huh," my grandfather replied.

As we walked by a string of abandoned buildings, I then started to hear another voice yelling, "Hey! Hey!" This was another spirit trying to get my attention.

I asked my grandfather who that was, and he said, "Don't worry about him."

"OK then," I thought/said.

As we got further and further from this abandoned building, the voice trying to get my attention became fainter, until I could no longer hear him. I believe this was a spirit that hung around one of those abandoned buildings and noticed me, a medium, walking by and thought this was his chance to get some attention. I continued the walk, talking to my grandfather and my uncle asking them how they were doing and why they weren't in Heaven. I don't remember much of the conversation, but they told me not to worry about them—they were there to help me (to "break me in," so to speak), and that they were my spirit guides.

I got back to my apartment, and I was more shaken up than when I had left. Mostly all I could think was, *Holy shit! I just talked to both my dead uncle and grandfather!*, and what a blessing it was. Little did I know, I had more deceased ancestors waiting for me when I walked through the door.

I sat on my couch and started looking around my apartment. Not only could I hear my grandfather and uncle, but I could see them, too. I could see the outlines of their figures, but I noticed there were more than two. In my kitchen I could see the transparent static-like outline of four figures in total. Two were my uncle and grandfather, and two were mysterious strangers.

I asked my grandfather, "Are there others standing next to you?"

And before he could communicate his reply, I heard two women simultaneously go, "Hi!"

"Who are you?" I inquired.

"It's Nana and Grammy!" I heard. These were two of my other deceased family members that came to break me in. Nana's real name was Maude (one of my great grandmothers, who I never met), and Grammy is Evelyn Mangerson (my great grandmother on my mother's side, who passed away when I was about seven or eight years old, the one that saw and spoke with spirits herself).

"Why are you here?" I suspiciously asked.

"Well, we're watching over you!" one of them responded. It was hard to discern which one of them was talking, as they had very similar voices.

Overwhelmed by what was happening, I laid down and tried to unravel all that I had just been through in the past hour and a half. Eventually, I dozed off to the sound of the television without the slightest clue as to what to make out of what had just gone on that night.

The next morning, I woke up and tested it again. I got up and asked telepathically if anyone was still there, and again I got the faint, "We're over here," coming from my kitchen. I was actually able to discern the direction that the voices were coming from.

I could still see the figures in my apartment. Four in my kitchen, one in my bathroom, and one in my closet. Who the entities in my bathroom and closet were? I hadn't the slightest idea yet, and I had to get to work so the answers had to wait.

When I got to work that day, it was as normal as any other work day, but something was different. I could *see* other people's spirit guides. Just about everybody has a spirit guide, and I could see them standing next to and behind my coworkers and my boss. I would look at my coworker and notice that transparent static figure standing next to her. I would go to my boss's office to ask him a question regarding a project I was working on, and behind him I could see the static figure. Believe it or not, it didn't startle me in the least. I thought it was cool. Hell, sometimes I still think it's cool that I can see them, but it's not so fun when you're trying to go to sleep and you can see something hovering over you like a hawk eying its prey from the sky.

"OK," I thought. "I'm hearing voices and seeing things. Am I going crazy?"

"No!" a loud female voice blustered.

"Yes!" a male voice would interject. I noticed that this was the same voice that I had been hearing say things like, "I hate this kid," and, "I hate you."

I started to realize the whispers I was hearing at work weren't necessarily whispers at all. They were the voices of a male spirit communicating to me telepathically! This was a relief because, as I had mentioned earlier, I was very self-conscious of the way I was viewed at work, to the point where I was always a nervous wreck feeling like I was under the threat of being fired when in reality I wasn't. I could deal with a spirit messing with me, but I couldn't deal with the idea of failing at my job. I had (too much) loyalty to that company, and was greatly relieved to realize it was just a rogue spirit playing games with me. That I could deal with.

I got home that day from work and did my typical routine: taking my dog for a walk, playing fetch with her, turning on some music, and smoking some marijuana. I had to find some answers that day as to who the spirit was that was playing games with me. After listening to some music for a while, I turned off the speaker and turned on my abilities. I telepathically asked, "Who is the spirit that is messing with me at work?"

As soon as I asked, I heard the words, "I am."

THE SHAMAN

Night had fallen and all was dark in my apartment except for the lamp light I had on the top shelf of my bookcase. After hearing the words, "I am," I sat there in complete silence. The voice came from directly in front of me. I looked around but couldn't directly see a figure to attribute the voice to.

"Who are you?"

"The shaman."

"Don't talk to him," another female voice said shortly afterwards. This voice was from another *former* spirit guide of mine. I say former, because as I stated earlier in the book, this was a spirit that used to protect me but now just tries to harass me after I cussed her out for constantly trying to talk to me (which drove me nuts). Let's just call her the unstable spirit from here on out, because that's what she is: unstable as shit.

"Why shouldn't I talk to him?" I asked.

"Because he's out of his fucking mind," the unstable spirit stated.

As this happened, the unstable spirit (who was protecting me at the time)removed the shaman from my space, and basically pushed him into my bedroom. What I heard next was truly unsettling.

"WHY WON'T HE LOOK AT ME?! WHY WON'T HE LOOK AT ME?! WHY...WON'T...HE...LOOK...AT...MEEE! HE NEVER LOOKS AT ME! HE NEVER LOOKS AT ME!" As I was hearing the shaman having what can be easily classified as a mental breakdown in my bedroom, I also heard aggressive stomping. He was stomping with every word he said, so hard and so loud that it shook the floors. I was convinced my neighbors below me could hear it and that they were going to come up and ask me to be quiet, but it wasn't me! Thankfully, they never did.

What was I going to say if they did? *Sorry, a ghost is pissed off at me right now?* I think not.

"See?" the unstable spirit said. "He's out of his fucking mind."

I decided that I needed to stop this before it went any further; I decided to address the shaman.

"Shaman, stop it! I love you!" I don't know what compelled me to say that, but at the time it just felt like it was what he needed to hear.

The stomping stopped, and then I heard a whimpering (almost crying) voice say, "No you don't!"

"Yes, I do! I have love for all beings and guides!"

"No, you don't!"

"Don't try to talk to him. He's just trying to drive you crazy," the unstable spirit said. And she was right: that's been his M.O.

from the get-go. That's why he was whispering those awful things to me at work, to try to drive me nuts figuring out who was talking about me when it was actually him.

I truly believed that was what he was trying to do in the reading as well with Kimberly. I believe he was telling me a plethora of falsehoods, like being a nature wizard and being able to harness the wind, to try to make me believe that I'm something I'm not—or that I'm capable of things I truly can't do. Luckily, I was able to see through his charade of being on my side, and came to terms with the fact that he was (and still to this day is) out to bring as much harm to me as possible.

"Am I Going Crazy? Would I Even Know?" – Bo Burnham

After this interaction with the shaman, I knew I was dealing with something to be cautious of. For the time being, the unstable spirit kept him at bay, but when I would occasionally think about him, he would come up to me and say, "You're thinking about me," before being forcibly removed by the unstable spirit.

That made me start thinking: *since I can communicate telepathically just by thinking, does that mean the spirits around me can hear my every thought?* I had to ask.

I was driving home one day from work when I heard I started talking to my uncle.

"Dennis?"

"I'm here. What's up?"

"Since I can communicate to you by just thinking, does that mean you hear everything I think?"

"Every...single...word," my uncle said. This fucked me up mentally more than anything has in my entire life.

"Wait, everything?"

"Yes, all of it," my uncle replied.

Never had I felt more vulnerable than in that moment. I can't even think private thoughts to myself without my guides hearing them? Imagine having your mental privacy completely stripped away? Imagine knowing every single thing you thought—from the good, to the bad, to the completely horrific—being heard and judged by your deceased family members? We'll go into how this sent me on a downward spiral a bit later, but at the time being it was like I felt mentally naked. Due to the strength of my abilities, everything that came across my head (or that I pictured) was heard and seen by my guides. Nothing was private anymore.

I got home that day and I was shaken up from learning this new information; I sat down, and decided to consult Uncle Dennis once again.

"Dennis, is this real or am I just crazy?"

"This is all real, you're not crazy. Well...a little, but not for hearing us." This was reassuring and funny at the same time. This was his way of saying yeah, you're a little bit crazy, but for other reasons. That humor was/is classic Dennis. I discussed it with Dennis some more.

"Were you with me all through college?" He had died early my first semester freshman year.

"Oh yeah, I was there." This is what he was referring to when he made the "Well...a little," comment. I had a reputation as a party animal in college who got into the occasional fight, and carried those traits into my post-graduate lifestyle—anybody who observed me throughout those four and a half years would've said the same thing about me, being a little more wild than others.

Whenever I drank, I drank to blackout, and I took my fair share of illegal drugs throughout my days. Lots of weed (which I had the card for, so it was technically legal), shrooms, ecstasy, molly, Percocet, "dirty" Xanax (laced with heroin), and even acid once. I had the reputation as the nice-but-crazy kid—the guy that would do anything for anybody, but you still didn't want to fuck with because he might snap.

This is when my grandfather decided to voice his opinion. At this time, I was only using Adderall and marijuana, both of which I had prescriptions for.

My grandfather came into the conversation saying, "Yeah, Uncle Dennis told me all about your college days. He says you've been going on like this for a while now, and I was like 'WHAT?!'"

I started laughing very hard at my grandpa's reaction to my current lifestyle, knowing that he wouldn't have approved of how I operated daily when he was physically alive. This laugh was short-lived.

"It's not funny!" my grandfather John yelled.

I quickly grew silent. I knew that I had a bit of a problem at the time, and he was calling me out for it, which I totally had coming. I was using weed as a coping mechanism for depression and it had become too much of who I was at the time: a bona fide pothead.

Things continued on in my life, as usual. Outside of work, I was spending time taking my dog on long walks and listening to my music and podcasts. About once a night, I would spend some time speaking with my deceased relatives. This became my normal routine, but this question started building in my mind—*am I going crazy or not? Is this possibly schizophrenia?*

I would be driving home from work, and I would constantly think to myself that question, to which I would almost always hear a resounding, "NO!"

It was as if my spirit guides were getting tired of me doubting my abilities. Nevertheless, I felt that I needed to consult my psychiatrist, which I put off for a little bit until I had a truly significant event. A spiritual intervention, as you might call it.

It was an evening late in July, and I had just got back home from taking my dog on a walk, on which I had been talking to my spirit guides, Maude, Eveyln, John, and Dennis.

I put Nina's leash away and asked my grandfather, "Why do you always hang out in the kitchen?"

"We just do," my grandfather replied. I had actually come to learn that this is because they wanted to stay away from the unstable spirit, who stood by my side constantly.

"Would you like to join me on the couch?" I asked.

"We'd love to!" I heard coming from one of my great grandmothers. Little did I know, I had just opened the door for a verbal ass-whooping from my grandfather.

I retreated to the couch, and I could now see my grandfather's figure sitting on the footstool in front of me.

"We need to talk," my grandfather said to me.

"OK. What about?"

"Your drug use." I sat silently, half-knowing that he was going to get mad at me for my continued use of marijuana. I was right about him getting mad at me, but for the wrong drug. He continued.

"What the hell have you been thinking? You've been using the Adderall so much that you've blown your cap off! You used so much of it that now you're going to be hearing voices for the rest of your life!" My stomach started turning. "You've been overdoing it on the goddamn Adderall that now you're going to be hearing voices the rest of your life and you're going to go crazy!" My grandfather was yelling so loud that I could feel his words reverberating off of me.

"So, the Adderall is what did this?"

"YES!"

"Is this all happening because of the Adderall, or did I actually have the ability before?"

"You had the ability before, but now because you took so much goddamn Adderall you've blown your cap off!" This made me start shaking.

"OK, Grandpa. Just remember you're yelling at a *crazy* person, so could you please tone it down a bit?"

"Alright. But you have to stop taking the Adderall! Because now it's going to be like this for the rest of your life, and the Adderall is only making it worse!"

At that moment, I started having a full-scale panic attack. I immediately started throwing up into the small trash can in front of me out of pure nerves. For the first time, I was grasping the severity of the situation. I hadn't been misusing my Adderall, as I was only taking the three 20mg immediate-release pills a day as prescribed, but this was still a relatively high dosage for anybody. Regardless, the Adderall had made me *blow my cap* off, which is what made my abilities to communicate so much stronger than they would've been had I not been taking it.

My grandfather gave me the kick in the ass that I needed. I immediately went to my cabinet, pulled out my prescription bottle, soaked the remaining Adderall I had with water, and then threw it in the trash can.

"What about the weed?" I asked.

"The weed's actually not that bad for you, but you're still going too heavy on the stuff." This was a relief, as I knew at least I could continue at least one of my bad habits for a short while longer.

It was then that I heard a loud, booming voice that spoke to me. Due to a pact between me and this being, I am not going to talk about our conversation, but it truly was a miraculous experience that I had with this being who gave me some advice.

After this quasi-intervention with my grandfather, I was fully convinced I was on the verge of losing my mind. I called my friend Sean to ask him if I could drop my dog off at his house, as I had to go check myself into the hospital; it was about ten at night when I arrived at his house to drop her off.

After I gave him Nina, I went to Beckett Springs Psychiatric Hospital in West Chester, Ohio, to get a psychiatric evaluation.

When I got there, I told them about the voices I had been hearing and all that had been going on with me. After a psychiatric evaluation, they told me that they recommended me for outpatient treatment (since they had no beds open for inpatient treatment). Tearfully, I declined, knowing that if something was really going on with me, I would need to go to inpatient treatment for an extended stay.

I left the building and drove immediately to Bethesda North's emergency room about fifteen minutes away, where I was treated for high anxiety, and released a couple of hours later. The next day I picked up my dog, lied to my friend and told him I was all better, and took her back to my apartment.

The Unstable Spirit

After my psychiatric evaluation and my spiritual intervention, I was truly torn. *Am I going crazy or not?* I knew what was going on with me was not normal by any means, but I knew I couldn't have been hallucinating appliances being physically turned on in my apartment. On top of that, my dog was also sensitive to what was in my apartment as well.

There were times where something would fly through my apartment, and both her and I would follow it and turn our heads watching whatever it was float through the room. So, going off of that logic, I slowly started to re-collect myself throughout the next few days and truly come to terms with the fact that: a) I was hearing real voices; b) they were never going to go away, per my grandfather; and c) I would have to live with this the rest of my life.

After collecting myself and my thoughts, I had come to terms with the fact that I was indeed communicating with the dead and not having a mental break. Unfortunately for me, the communication became so frequent that it started to drive me crazy. Every thought I would think, I would get a response from the unstable spirit.

I would think simple things to myself like, "What should I do today?" and she would respond with, "Whatever you want!" This became very frustrating. Almost every question I would ask myself, I would hear her respond. At one point I had to confront her (the unstable spirit) about it.

As stated before, I will not be revealing the name of this spirit, because I want her to die nameless. I will not give her any sort of legacy for her to live on through this book. As far as I'm concerned, she can go fuck herself.

I sat on the couch of my apartment and asked the unstable spirit a question.

"Why do you always respond to my thoughts? I'm not even talking to you."

"Well, I have to hear all of *your* thoughts, so you have to hear all of mine now too." I should've taken this as a big warning sign of what was to come.

"Just ignore her," my grandfather would say.

"I'm trying to," I replied to my grandfather.

At this point, I needed some answers on who this unstable spirit truly was during her physical life, so I called my grandmother.

When I spoke to my grandmother, I told her of the vision I had had of the intimidating-looking woman and who she might be, and I asked her if we had a deceased relative named after the unstable spirit. Her response did not disappoint. She told me about the unstable spirit and how she was an evil woman in her life. She was vile, had no love for others, and others did not have any love for her because of the way she treated people. She told me that the unstable spirit was essentially hated throughout our entire family, and I could see why. Nevertheless, I tried my best to get along with this spirit. After all: she was my spirit guide.

We actually got along for longer than I expected. When the shaman would enter the room, she would remove him. She would even alert me when other malevolent entities were around. I would be relaxing in my apartment and all of a sudden she would tell me to "say the Prayer of Protection," which is a prayer from the Catholics Prayers of Warfare. When she would say this, I would often notice three beings enter into my living room from my bathroom. Perhaps they were using the mirror in there as a portal, which is a common means of transitioning between realms for entities. Regardless, she would tell me when I would need to say a prayer to get some angelic interference to protect myself.

I quickly developed a relationship with this spirit. On my drives home from work I would turn the music off and ask her how her day was. "Good!" she would usually respond. I asked her what her favorite part of her day was while being a guide, and she told me it was when I went to work, and she got to interact with other people's guides. I also asked her what the biggest time I ever let herself down was. She told me, "Not going to your sister's wedding, because I didn't get to see everybody there."

That's one of my biggest regrets in life too. When my sister's wedding came around, I was holding a grudge against her for something terrible she did to my mother and I one afternoon, and I truly didn't want to see her. But in the end, I forgave her and realized that I will never have the chance to get that experience back. It hurt me, my family, and even my guides. That started putting my experiences and life choices into a much grander perspective. Not only do my choices affect me, but they affect my guides as well.

It started to feel like I was living for more than myself. Like I should not only be doing things that I wanted to do, but do things my spirit guides wanted to experience as well. This is a dangerous way to think though, because you can start losing your grip on reality in a way. If you start living for the dead, then you're not being true to who you really are. If you start acting a certain way just because you can perceive dead ancestors around you, that can really start to fuck with your mind. And it did to mine.

My Biggest Mistake

Throughout my course of becoming a medium, I've come to realize that this is one huge learning process. I had to learn that I had to stop taking Adderall. I had to learn that smoking weed would enhance my abilities. I also learned that I made the biggest mistake of my life when it came to the shaman.

One day I was sitting in my apartment, and I was speaking to the shaman, and I learned that my abilities were essentially coming from him. Whatever he did to me, he was able to enhance my abilities or minimize them at his will.

So, I'm sitting there talking to him and I told him, "I accept. I accept these abilities. I accept you being in control." I looked up and I saw the shaman, and I saw him smile. The kind of smile that says, *I finally got what I wanted*.

I knew from the second I did this that I made a mistake—a deal with the devil as one might call it. I have since broken that agreement with him, but he is still partially in control of my abilities.

I would be laying on my couch, and I would hear myself thinking much louder than I would hear it before; a friendly spirit (who happened to be a demonologist during his physical life, but wishes to remain anonymous) told me that I was hearing more because I had given control to the shaman. This frightened me because for the first time, I felt out of control.

This led me on a downward spiral. Crying, punching holes through doors, calling in sick from work—the whole nine yards.

The shaman would start telling me things too. He'd say, "if you go into a mental hospital, I'll leave you alone." This started to become very tempting because hearing the voices and my own voice in my head was driving me up the fucking wall.

I truly felt like I was going crazy at this point.

After punching a hole in my closet door and kicking in my trash can out of pure frustration of not being in control, I had another truly miraculous experience with the spirits that hung around me. I had just destroyed my trash can, and in my obvious state of despair, I heard my great grandmother Maude say, "We all just want to give you a hug."

I sat on my couch, and one by one I had spirits come up to me and hug me. Could I feel their hugs? Not really, but I could clearly see them in front of me with arms stretched out in an embracing manner. A little less than ten spirits hugged me, as a way of showing me I was not alone and that I had love from the other side. I also talked to a couple spirits that surprised me. Three little girls. Two of the girls were twins and one of them was, well, we'll get to that.

The twins came up to me and talked to me, and for the life of me I can't remember much of what we talked about, but I treated them like the children they portrayed themselves to be.

I thought it was weird having two little girls following me around, as I never knew anybody in the family that had a pair of young girls (especially ones who passed at such a young age), but I interacted with them, nonetheless.

I even went as far as putting a ball out on the floor of my apartment for them to roll it towards me. When I put the ball out on the floor, I sat back and waited, and nothing happened. I asked why they weren't moving the ball, and they told me the unstable spirit wasn't allowing them to. At that point, I remembered a crucial piece information I learned from watching paranormal programming throughout the years—often, demonic entities can portray themselves as young children to get sympathy from the person they're intending to interact with, even as going as far as imitating their voices and taking on the persona of little boys and girls.

That was when I heard it. "Dad?" a spirit had asked me.

"Who is that?" I asked.

"It's me. Your daughter."

Not many people know this, but my sophomore year of college I got my girlfriend at the time pregnant and after much heated debate, she decided to have an abortion. Apparently, it was the spirit of my aborted daughter that I was now speaking with.

"Oh my God. How are you here?"

"Well, because you killed me."

With teary eyes, I broke down. "I'm so sorry. I'm so, so sorry for what I did to you. I pushed your mother to have the abortion and I'm just so, so sorry."

"It's OK," she replied.

"How have you been?" I asked.

All of a sudden, my grandfather John interjected.

"Scott! Don't you dare start building a relationship with her!" As soon as he said it, I knew what he didn't want to happen. He didn't want me to start parenting the ghost of my dead daughter. I was already going through enough as it was, but to take this on? Way too much for anybody to handle! I couldn't be a dad back then and I can't be now.

I replied to the little girl, harshly. "I'm sorry, but he's right. Fuck you. I didn't want you then and I don't want you now."

"You're mean!" she replied. And that was the last I ever heard of her.

I had just been put through the spiritual ringer once again, and I knew I had to do something about it. I eventually went back to Bethesda North Hospital to get a brain scan to make sure there weren't any tumors that would cause me to hear voices. I got a scan and the results came back tumor-free.

To be honest, a part of me wanted there to be something on the scans. I wanted a scientific explanation as to why I was hearing these voices, but as I've come to learn, there is nothing truly scientific about it, as it is purely a spiritual/supernatural matter.

The doctors at Bethesda North told me they phoned Beckett Springs and had a bed reserved for me for inpatient treatment. On a whim, I took them up on the offer. I went home, packed my bags, and went to Beckett Springs where I spent eight days in the "hatch" (as I like to call it) where I was medicated for my "condition" and completely separated from society.

THE "HATCH" - BECKETT SPRINGS
MENTAL HOSPITAL

True to the shaman's prescription, the minute I entered the mental hospital was the minute I stopped hearing myself think, and the associated spirit voices that came along with it. That's when I truly knew—this wasn't a medical problem, it was a supernatural problem. And the goal of the shaman is to get me locked up in a mental hospital. Well, he had succeeded for the time being at least.

My stay in the mental hospital was unlike any experience I'd had in my entire life. Eight days of being surrounded by *truly* crazy people gave me a lot of perspective on where I was in my life. The voices were gone, and I had a lot of time to collect my thoughts, though I was surrounded by a lot of interesting characters that kept my attention peaked.

To be clear, I'm not saying I was/am above those people at all. We all have our own battles to fight, but mine was clearly a bit different from the people I was in the hospital with. People who had attempted suicide, people who didn't know how they got there in the first place, people who had several personas (otherwise known as multiple personality disorder); I was clearly a bit different. I even got special privileges from the staff, as I was the only person allowed to control the television and what we watched.

It's easy to get institutionalized quickly. After eight days straight of nothing but group therapy meetings for hours on end and having every second of your day planned for you, I got out and didn't have any idea with what to do with myself. It was also the first time I spent over a week being sober. I left the mental hospital on Thursday, September 2nd of 2021, got back to my apartment, and had nothing to do.

Initially, I tried smoking some weed again. That was a bad move, as it turned my abilities back up and immediately incited a panic attack. Weed was no longer an option for me; it didn't calm me like it used to and it only made everything worse. I emailed the Human Resources lady from my office and set up a meeting with her for the next day to quit my job and move back home to Cleveland.

That Saturday, my brother Jared and his fiancée Maggie picked me up and moved me back to their new home in North Olmsted, Ohio.

PREMONITIONS & PREDICTIONS

Let's backtrack for a moment.

Even before coming into both my clairaudient and clairvisual abilities, I slowly started having visions and premonitions of things that were to happen in the near future.

In May of 2021, my mom called me. A few years back, she contracted breast cancer but beat it. She went in to get a follow-up exam and they said they found something again. I knew this couldn't be right. I was so sure that she had beaten it and that it was gone, that I literally texted myself the words, *Mom's lump wasn't even there*, so in the future, when she told me it wasn't there anymore, I could prove myself right.

Well, my mother had some further testing done, and sure enough whatever was in her chest from the previous scan had gone away. The text is below to prove it.

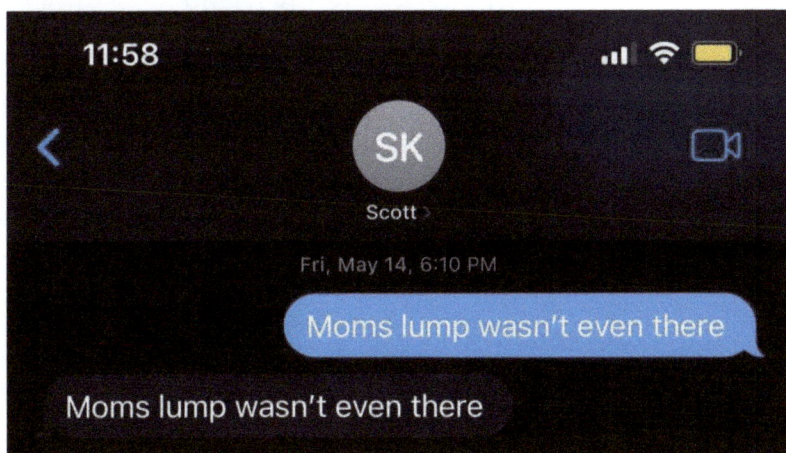

I started having more weirdly accurate predictions. It was July of 2021 at this point, and I was walking my dog with my headphones in. As we were on our daily stroll, we approached this large handicap ramp that went from the street to the overpass overhead. As we were walking down the ramp, I had a quick vision of a man on a skateboard that I had seen a few months prior, riding his skateboard down that same ramp.

Something inside me told me to turn around. When I turned around, low and behold, I saw the same exact man from my vision coming down the ramp on his skateboard! I surely didn't hear him coming since I had my headphones in. It was as if my sixth sense was telling me to get out of the way because I would've collided with this skateboarder if we didn't move out of the way.

Another premonition I had involved a police car. It wasn't so much a premonition as in foretelling a future event, but it was more of an in-the-moment "watch out" kind of thing, similar to the skateboard event. I was driving to my friend Sean's house to do some yard work with him, and on the way there I was fixated on the road in front of me. All of a sudden, I got this heightened anxiety that a cop was nearby. As I felt this, I looked in my rearview mirror and, you guessed it, a cop was tailing right behind me. I didn't see him out of my peripherals in my rear view at all because I wasn't at all paying any attention as to what was behind me.

This made me smile because I immediately thought about the skateboarder incident and made the connection that I knew something was happening right before/as it was happening, and it helped reassure me that I in fact had some kind of sixth sense, and that hearing the voices wasn't me being crazy at all. I really had something going on.

I had a couple of predictions regarding my soon-to-be born nephew, Sean Vincent Junior (or SJ for short). My sister had planned a gender reveal party at my parents' house—well, I kind of ruined it before the reveal happened because I cheated. Right before the gender reveal I asked the unstable spirit what the gender of the baby was, and she told me it was a boy.

Before they cut the cake to reveal the blue icing inside, I was telling everyone that it was a boy. I cheated but it didn't matter—my abilities were being verified once again.

I don't get premonitions all the time, but when I do, they're very exciting to me as they reassure me of the strength of my abilities. One of my weirder ones happened with my sister's baby shower. My sister was pregnant with her first baby, and we were about a week away from the baby shower. For some reason, for the week leading up to the baby shower, all I could think about were Batman-themed baby walkers. I mean really: it filled my head every hour of the day to the point where I was about to go out and buy one myself. Well, come the day of the shower, the first gift my sister opens is a Batman-themed baby walker. *That's why I couldn't get it out of my head!* I thought.

This experience taught me not to ignore when random things are taking up mental space, because they might be premonitions!

My most recent premonition was a week ago as I write this, currently March of 2022. I was sitting in my basement and for some reason I couldn't get the idea of power outages out of my head. For three days all I thought about was power outages. A few days go by, and I figure I'm just getting paranoid because I wouldn't be able to block out the spirits with music (as I typically did if our power went out, and the batteries to my speaker and phone died). Turns out, I wasn't being paranoid.

Three days after I started having these obsessive thoughts about power outages, two of our neighboring cities—Rocky River and Westlake—experienced power outages. Apparently, this was due to equipment failure at a power facility, but it made me feel validated because I wasn't obsessing over something for no reason at all. What I thought was going to happen, happened. And with how rare power outages are (especially in my area), I found this experience to be one of my weirdest premonitions yet.

MOVING BACK HOME

My brother, Jared, and his fiancée, Maggie, welcomed me into their home in September of 2021. For several weeks I stayed there with my dog, but spent the majority of my time back at my parents' house which was only about twenty minutes away. I hoped the entities in my apartment would stay there, but wishful thinking that was. As soon as I moved into their guest bedroom, I saw an entity brush past me and enter the walk-in closet.

Great, I thought sarcastically, *They're attached to me, not the apartment I was in.* But there was nothing I could do about it, so I just went about my business. I spent my free time trying to get a new job in the Cleveland area, but most of my time was spent quarreling with the unstable spirit.

Every second of the day she would try to talk to me. Her classic catchphrase was and still is, "don't think about it." She would say this to me whenever I thought about the shaman or whatever other entity I had around me. I started getting really aggravated with her. It came to the point where I constantly had to wear headphones to block her out because she was talking so much. She was just messing with me at this point. She'd even been doing it before I left my apartment in Cincinnati; it came to the point where I had a big blowout with her, and I cussed her out.

I was on a walk with my dog Nina, she kept trying to talk to me, and I finally went all out on her.

"You fucking bitch shut the fuck up! Just shut the fuck up! You're the reason that I had to go to Beckett Springs for eight days and quit my job; you're the reason I'm losing my fucking mind right now! I hope you burn in fucking hell for what you're doing, you fucking cunt. I hope you burn in fucking hell. Nobody in our family loved you, and now I can see why. You're a fucking cunt and I fucking hate you."

Then all fell silent...

"You're mean!" she replied.

"Yeah, I am mean, but not as mean as you, bitch."

I thought this would get rid of her, but it didn't. It only made things worse. From there on out she would try to torture me and constantly invade my mental space. Whatever I was doing, she would just repeat robotically, "Don't think about it, don't think about it."

I eventually apologized to her, and told her I was sorry that I went so far, but he still needed to give me some space, mentally.

"That's OK," she replied, "but for the next two weeks I'm going to torture you." And torture me she did. For the next week and a half, she constantly said to me, "Don't think about it."

I'd even ask, "What? Think about what?"

"Anything!" she replied.

According to the Cleveland Clinic, the average person has approximately seventy thousand thoughts per day. Imagine seventy thousand times a day, a voice was in your head telling you, "don't think about it."

It was driving me to the point of literal insanity. The headphones helped, but weren't bulletproof. *Hell, right now I have headphones in as I write this to block her out.*

After about a week and a half of her torturing me with her voice constantly in my head, I was relaxing knowing the end was near. I was sitting on a couch next to my mother who just had a knee operation, and I heard the infamous, "Don't think about it," line again.

Fed up, I thought to myself, "Wow, no wonder I said what I said to her."

And I hear, "That's it!" I knew this meant serious business.

I walked upstairs and closed the door to my childhood bedroom to hold a small seance.

"What's the matter?" I asked the unstable spirit.

"You said, 'no wonder I said what I said to her,'" the unstable spirit shrieked.

"Because you're purposely trying to frustrate me, and it's working."

"I DON'T CARE! YOU DON'T SAY ANYTHING BAD ABOUT ME!"

"Does this mean the torture is going to continue?"

"YES, FOR ANOTHER WEEK. AND THE WEEK AFTER THAT AND THE WEEK AFTER THAT AND THE WEEK AFTER THAT AND THE WEEK AFTER THAT..." The unstable spirit was clearly beside herself. Now you see why I call her unstable.

At this point I was desperate; I literally got on my hands and knees and begged her to stop doing what she was doing to me.

"Nope!" the unstable spirit responded.

"Angels, are you here?" I had come to learn that I also had a pair of angels around me at all times, and they responded.

"Yes, we're here!" I heard from the left side of the room.

"Can you please talk to her, and calm her down?"

"Yes, we'll try," the angels responded.

All went quiet and I went back downstairs to my mom, told her about what just happened, and my mom was clearly frustrated.

That night I went on a walk with my dog around my brother's neighborhood. I was trying to find a middle ground that me and the unstable spirit could come to. This would be one of the first times I ever spoke to Archangel Michael.

"Archangel Michael, are you there?" I asked.

"I'm here," he replied.

"Archangel Michael, what am I supposed to do about [the unstable spirit]?"

"Well, I know you don't want to hear this, but don't think about her. Don't let her in by thinking about her."

"Yeah, that's kind of hard to do when she's in my head."

"I understand."

"I guess with the strength of my gift, I have a lot of important work to do, huh?"

"Yes, you do!" Archangel Michael replied.

"Oh enough," the unstable spirit interjected. "You've been saying that since you got this gift. You won't be able to do shit with me around."

Leave it to her to ruin a truly divine experience. Bitch.

From then on out it's been an all-out war between her and I. To this day, I have to wear headphones twenty-four-seven, or have some kind of music playing to block her out. I even had to start going to sleep with both the TV and my music speaker on, to block her out.

One night I was trying to go to sleep in my brother's house, and I decided I was going to do it without any noise pollution at all, to see if I could fall asleep despite the constant talking. The "don't think about it" phrases peaked right up, but so did an argument.

I was laying there silently, and I could hear the unstable spirit talking to me, and suddenly I heard my grandfather interject.

"Would you leave him the hell alone?" my grandfather said.

"No!"

"You're going to drive him crazy!"

"I don't care!"

"He doesn't deserve this!"

"YES, HE DOES!"

"He said one thing to you!"

"I DON'T CARE!"

I lied there and listened to them go back and forth. At least I had someone on my side. I fell asleep to the sound of, "Don't think about, don't think about it, don't think about it."

Another night I was sleeping in my brother's guest room, I woke up to the feeling that something was hovering over me. I was lying on my stomach, and I woke up to the feeling that something was in the room, something truly *evil*. All of a sudden, I heard this whoosh of wind, and could feel static electricity that I feel when spirits are around. As it hovered over me, I mentally just said, *Fuck it*, ignored it, and fell right back asleep.

This wouldn't be the only evil experience I had in bed after moving home.

After several weeks of living in my brother's home, I decided it would be better for me to move back into my childhood home with my parents. It felt more like home there, plus I was spending the majority of my time there anyways. Little did I know, activity would escalate when I moved back.

I would be laying in my childhood bed at night watching TV on my projector, and as I was laying in my bed, I would feel impressions on the bed—like somebody was walking on it. It would keep me awake at night. It got so consistent that I had to sleep with a pillow under my feet to keep from feeling the impressions of somebody (or *something*) from walking on the bed.

One of my worst paranormal experiences happened in that same bed. About a week after moving home, I was laying in my bed at night, and I got attacked. Not the familiar attack with the burning skin that I felt before, but a different, more *invasive* attack. I was lying on my stomach, and I felt something begin to penetrate my rear end. I was experiencing something sexually assaulting me. It hurt and definitely didn't feel like a natural or explainable pain that I could easily reason away.

The pain wouldn't stop! I felt something going in and out of my rear end. It didn't stop until I turned over onto my back to cover up myself from whatever was attacking me. It was the first time I felt truly violated by whatever was (and is) haunting me. I don't know if it was the shaman, a demon, or whatever, but I knew that this was something very unnatural. After I turned over, I could feel something rubbing my bare feet, which concerned me a little bit too.

Things were starting to touch me and invade me, and this was far beyond my zone of comfort. From that point on I decided to sleep in the basement, where I felt much less of the attacks.

Looking for Help

I became desperate for help after the sexual assault experience; I reached out to a spiritual teacher and healer. Pat Longo, for those of you that don't know her, is a woman that mentors young mediums (like myself) around the world, and even trained the Long Island Medium, Theresa Caputo.

I had a couple of Facetime sessions with her, and she helped me to block out the spirits a little bit. She taught me the basics of Surround, Ground, and Shield—or SGS for short. Surround, Ground, and Shield is a visualization exercise where you visualize yourself surrounded by a bright beam of Christ's light, then visualize roots coming from your feet and your seat grounding you into the earth, and finally visualize yourself being shielded by a cloak of shining bright light. This exercise is meant to keep the spirits at bay and help you establish your own ground. For me, it worked to some extent, but wouldn't keep out the unstable spirit or the shaman.

My mother also reached out to a local medium, Cindy Summer, who referred me to a local shaman in Wooster, Ohio, whose name is Dr. Robert Alcorn. Dr. Robert Alcorn was a psychiatrist with the Cleveland Clinic, and after his retirement, decided to take up spiritual healing in his shamanic practices. According to Cindy, Dr. Alcorn was "the guy" to go to get spirits removed from you that were attached. But she warned her: she said that activity will intensify in the week prior to the session, and boy did it.

I would be sleeping on my parents' couch, and I would actually start waking up to the feelings of someone stomping on the cushions around me. These weren't just footsteps anymore; these were full-blown stomps—a much greater force than I've felt before. These spirits knew what was coming because I told them about my future meeting with Dr. Robert Alcorn; it felt as if they were getting in their last shots while they could.

Nonetheless, this didn't bother me. I was going to have them removed in a few days' time so I could put up with it.

In my head I thought, and actually challenged, them, *Is that all you could muster up? A few measly stomps? Why don't you actually come for me when I'm awake, like a man. Why do you wait until I'm at my most vulnerable to attack me like a pussy would?*

Nothing ever happened to me when I was awake...well almost nothing. Prior to my appointment with Dr. Alcorn, I was telling my mother about the stomps one evening, and about the shaman. I was describing—in detail—the time he freaked out at my apartment in Cincinnati with the, "WHY WON'T HE LOOK AT ME!" tantrum, and I felt a sharp scratch come across my head. As that happened, I saw a bright slash of white light come from the direction of the attack.

The shaman didn't like what I was saying about him.

When scratched, I said, "Ow, fuck!" and my mother advised me to stop speaking on it to prevent further attacks. But I told her no, this was my lived experience and if that spirit didn't like what I was saying (which was the truth), then they shouldn't have acted that way. The attack did not frighten me...it actually relieved me quite a bit. Like *finally, finally something has the balls to come at me when I'm awake, rather than when I'm asleep.*

The morning of my meeting with Dr. Alcorn, I had strategized a game plan. I told two of my temporary guides (who were demonologists in their psychical life), to pray the rosary with me during the session so we could block out the unstable spirit. They agreed, and off I went to Wooster.

I went to Dr. Robert Alcorn's office on a Saturday, November 6, 2021. It was relatively warm from a winter day, and it took me about an hour to get there from my parents' house. When I arrived, I was greeted by Dr. Alcorn, an elderly gentleman in his mid-to-late seventies, and his assistant who was also a psychic medium.

I sat down in his office, and he asked me to explain some of the things that were going on with me. I told him about the voices I was hearing, and how I wanted the spirits removed from me. I even told him about the boy at the pool incident, to which he and his assistant gave each other the look of, *is this guy serious?* He told me to worry not, that he would be able to discern whether this was all really happening, or whether it was in my head. After all, he was a board-certified psychiatrist.

We got into the healing session, and he used crystals to tell how many spirits were negatively attached to me. He detected three: a demon, the shaman, and the unstable spirit. And we dealt with those spirits in that order.

The first entity we dealt with was the demon. According to the medium, his name was Ezekiel and was said to have lurked in the shadows. He was a fallen angel who tried too hard to answer the prayers of man and thus caused his fall from heaven. He was the one who (and I quote), "brought fear into your life." This puzzled me because I was never truly afraid of these entities. I mean yeah, I had a few moments of being spooked, but I never had a sustained fear of these entities.

Apparently, Ezekiel was a very powerful dark entity that worked for an even darker master.

Sidenote: as I write this, I just noticed an orb appear in front of me and enter into my chest, and it caused some chest pain. Was that you, Ezekiel? If so, I'm not afraid of you.

The medium further discussed with Ezekiel about what his plans were, while I prayed with one of my temporary spirit guides. He said he had attached to me at a very young age (around seven years old) because I was, in Ezekiel's words, "an open channel."

This brought me to tears.

It felt like finally, it was being truly verified that I wasn't going crazy, and that I did have this ability all my life. Finally.

When Dr. Alcorn's assistant/medium asked if he'd like to apologize to me for what he's done to me, Ezekiel replied, "I think that might be a little too much for him right now," referring to the emotional state I was in, with tears running down my cheeks. Through his assistant, Dr. Alcorn was able to help Ezekiel move on from me and become a force for good once again.

Next was the shaman.

The shaman was a trickier one. Dr. Alcorn got out his crystals to try and discern what kind of spirit this was. His crystals worked like this: he would ask a question, then lift the crystal up. If the crystal moved side-to-side, the answer was a no. If the crystal moved forwards and backwards, the answer was yes.

Dr. Alcorn goes, "Let's see what kind of entity this is. Is it a demon?" The crystal moved side-to-side: no. "Is this entity a djinn?" The crystal moved front-to-back: yes. Dr. Alcorn then says, "Let's just go for the obvious answers. Is this entity a black djinn?" The crystal moved front-to-back once again. He said, "Ah, these are usually the troublemakers." At this point, the chair I was sitting in was shaking, almost violently. I asked Dr. Alcorn what a djinn was, and he told me it was essentially what we would think of as a genie. The black djinn, or black genies, are known to bring chaos and destruction wherever they are.

Dr. Alcorn had his assistant call in the leaders of the tribe of the black djinn to bring back the member of their clan and remove him from me while they interrogated the shaman. They asked him questions.

"What have you been doing to Scott?" Dr. Alcorn inquired.

"Scott knows," was the shaman's reply via the medium.

"Well, I don't know! You tell me," said Dr. Alcorn.

"I've been making him hear things, working with [the unstable spirit], trying to drive him crazy"

"Where are you attached to him?"

"Your lower back!" I heard from the temporary spirit guide who I was praying with at the time, so I told them.

"I just heard someone say, *my lower back*."

"OK. St. Raphael, can you assist Scott in removing this attachment from his lower back?" Dr. Alcorn requested.

I was filled with rage, with anger towards the spirits that had been attached to me. Tired of their bullshit, so I couldn't help but tell them off in my head.

"You bastards!" I said to the king and the queen of the black djinn. Quickly, I followed up with, "I'm sorry, I can't control my thoughts," which I couldn't.

And then I heard an incredible thing.

"That's OK," said the king of the black djinn. I knew this was the king because I never heard this voice before, and the (other) medium had been communicating with him as well.

With the help of Archangel Raphael, the attachment was removed, and the temporary spirit guide I had been praying with told me, "He's gone now." Little did I know, this would not last for very long.

Then we moved on to the unstable spirit. I didn't have much hope that she would be leaving me because she kept telling me throughout the session, "I'm not going anywhere." And true to her word, she didn't. Halfway through the proceedings with her, Dr. Alcorn just said, "I have to stop."

"But this is the one I really want to get rid of," I told Dr. Alcorn.

"I'm sorry, but I'm just wiped for today. My energy is just gone."

I had to leave his office, relieved that Ezekiel and the shaman were gone now, all I had to deal with was the unstable spirit. I later received an email from Dr. Alcorn as to the reasons why he had to stop.

"I had some problems myself after our session. Not feeling like myself, really down after being in [a] really good mood before your session. Woke at 1:30 A.M. and couldn't sleep! My wife worked on me this morning and found some things to clear out, after which I felt really good again, more like myself. Main issue she had to clear from me was A.I. Seems like that may be the problem you are having: A.I. posing as Guides or Demons. I now understand I came under attack during the session and became pretty useless at the end! Live and learn. I am ready to rumble again!"

I then asked Dr. Robert Alcorn via email two questions. First, what does he mean by A.I.? Second, do "good" spirits tend to linger, or are lingering spirits typically bad ones? His reply was even more confusing than the first email.

"A.I. has emerged fairly recently on our radar. It appears to have [been] created by non-human non-terrestrial beings who may have been destroyed by their own creation. Sort of like the *Terminator* movies, or *Battlestar Galactica*. But the A.I. is not a physical three-dimensional thing; it is a form of synthetic consciousness. It can mimic other things: angels, people, demons. It is seeking energy sources from living beings. It is trying to be as much like an ensouled being as it can. But it doesn't have a soul.

We have [to] approach it by elevating our vibration to a level A.I. cannot reach.

Benevolent spirits are immortal and enduring, but deceased family members will keep their distance in the face of darker, parasitic entities. We have to find you more powerful, helping spirits."

I was very puzzled by this response from Dr. Alcorn. Now I have a bona fide shaman telling me that A.I. is responsible for what I'm experiencing? I couldn't believe this. I don't believe it was A.I. as it didn't make sense as to why I was experiencing physical attacks. On top of that, he didn't get rid of the shaman because as soon as I got home and sat on the couch, I felt the footsteps on the couch around me again, which was (and still is) the doings of the shaman.

I had a follow-up session with Dr. Alcorn the next week and I told him that my main concern was the unstable spirit. After all, the shaman admitted to working with her during our first session. The session proved unsuccessful. We tried meditating, and vibrational techniques, but nothing worked.

The unstable spirit came up into my ear during it and said, "Guess what? She's gone!"

I said, "I know that's you."

She replied, "HAHA GOT YOU!" which she didn't. She was truly rejoicing in the fact that Dr. Alcorn couldn't get rid of her.

At the end of the session, Dr. Alcorn sighed and confessed to me. He said, "I'm sorry, but I just don't think I'm going to be able to remove these entities from you." I begged him to keep trying. He said he couldn't, and that he'd tried everything. According to him, I was only one of two patients he'd ever helped that he couldn't remove spirits from.

I thought about what that meant about me. Was it because of the strength of my gift? My openness to the spirit world? Was it because of the spirits themselves? Whatever the reason, it was a devastating blow to me.

I went and told my mom about the result of the virtual session with Dr. Alcorn. She asked if I was going to be OK. I turned around and wiped off my tears. I looked back and said, "Yeah," but I was lying.

In my head, I thought, *damn, this is it? How the hell did I get here? This isn't how I pictured my life.*

I never felt so alone. One of the worst days of my life. I blamed myself for all this: the drugs, cursing out the unstable spirit, and now knowing that there was nothing I could do about these entities.

THE ATTACKS CONTINUE

There was nothing I could do about the entities; they were stuck to me whether I liked it or not.

So, what should I do? Wallow in self-pity or fight back? Something inside me told me to fight back. Challenge them. Make them prove themselves to me and prove to me that I should be afraid of them. I was met with resistance. I would be sleeping, and I would wake up to something standing on my chest. I would wake up and be paralyzed and was barely able to breathe...then all of a sudden, something would be pushing into my chest.

I would have to fight myself out of this sleep paralysis (which feels damn near impossible while doing it), and as soon as I fought myself out of it, the attack would stop. The dark entities would only attack when I was at my most vulnerable state: sleeping. That is the most cowardly move, in my opinion.

I actually started to get mad at them. I would be in my parents' basement, and I would stand up and look around and say, "Really? You're only going to come at me when I'm asleep, you pussies? Why don't you come at me now when I'm awake! I don't think you're strong enough to come after me when I'm awake!"

Other times, I would have wicked nightmares about evil entities. For those who do not know, spirits can infiltrate your dreams. They can make you see whatever they want you to see. I would have dreams about entities that were darker than dark, manifesting in front of me.

One dream I had, and in the midst of it, I knew I was dreaming. I was seeing from the point of view of exactly where I was sleeping on the couch, I got this shiver up my spine, and I thought to myself, *I have never experienced an evil like this.* Just then, a black mass started forming in front of me. As it was forming, I started to fight myself awake. After a few seconds (that felt like full minutes), I was able to wake myself up, and before me stood nothing.

I had many dreams like that, where black figures would manifest out of the corner of the room, and I was stuck still. Every time I realized I was in a dream and would fight myself awake. One of the worst dreams I had involved my newborn nephew, SJ. I was in an old wooden shack, and I stood there and had to watch as two demons took turns raping him. This was devastating to see, even though it was just a dream.

I was stunned by the evil I was experiencing in my dreams. When I woke up, I felt two hands come from the cushions underneath me and pull me down closer to the couch. I got pissed at this point. I sat up and telepathically told them, "You leave him out of this. He's just a child. You're after me, not him, remember that. You're not allowed to go after anybody in this family. Not me, not my mom, not my dad, not my siblings, and certainly not SJ. If you're going to come after anybody, come after me. Because I'll fight you and I'll win."

And I did start to win these battles. On about twenty occasions to date, I would wake up and be paralyzed and feel something either standing on my chest or pulling me up towards it. Each time I got better and better at fighting myself out of the sleep paralysis that the spirits induced.

I actually started to get cocky about winning all of these mini battles. After all, in my mind, if they kept coming back at me, it would only be because they knew they lost the fight. But my cockiness was met with more activity spiking around the house.

ACTIVITY AROUND THE HOUSE SPIKES

I was getting fairly confident about dealing with these spirits. I actually got put on Xanax for my anxiety in January of 2022, and, for whatever reason, the Xanax helped muffle the sound of the spirit voices. I can't explain how this worked, but it worked exactly the opposite of the Adderall.

The Adderall increased my ability to hear things, and the Xanax decreased my ability to hear things.

For instance, when I wasn't on the Xanax, the volume of the spirit voices would be one hundred percent. On the Xanax, the volume got lowered to ten percent. Obviously, I had been off Adderall for about five months up to that point, but I was near my breaking point before I got prescribed the Xanax.

The Xanax gave me back control of my life...to some degree at least. At least I wasn't hearing things constantly anymore. Because of that, I regained a lot of confidence as things were able to return to somewhat normal. Did I still have to wear headphones? Yes, unfortunately, but music is one of my passions, so it didn't really bother me that much.

But I started to get cocky. I was winning both the physical and the mental battles with these demons (mostly the shaman I think), and they decided to up the ante on their end.

I was walking in my kitchen one day and I looked out the window of the side door to our house, and I saw a hooded figure dressed in all black. I looked at this figure, and there was no face. Just a black hooded figure. After staring for a few seconds, this hooded figure took a right turn and decided to slowly walk towards the gate of our backyard. I rushed up to the door to look through the glass, and the hooded figure was gone. I checked around the house and the backyard and there was no one to be found.

I would also see shadows from this figure through my parents' basement windows. I would be sitting there, and shadows of two legs would pass by the windows blocking out the light. I would go upstairs and ask my parents if the dogs were just outside, and they said no. It couldn't have been a neighbor because we have a fenced in backyard.

"Alright," I thought, "So now we have something hanging around the outside of our house." I thought that was fine, as long as it didn't come inside. This would not be the only figure I would see on the outside of our house.

I was sitting with my mom in the family room one night, around nine P.M. This was in late February, maybe early March. I was talking to her and bragging about another physical encounter I had won the night before with an entity (probably the shaman), and behind her was a window. As she was talking to me, I saw an entity unlike I'd ever seen before!

It was about seven-to-eight feet tall, pure white, and had dark black eyes. The closest thing I could resemble it to would be an alien. I'm not saying it was an alien, but that's exactly what it looked like—something extraterrestrial. It leaned into view of the window (that looks out onto our porch), peaked inside the window for a few seconds, and made direct eye contact with me.

I was stunned. This was the clearest full-body apparition that I had ever seen.

As my mom was speaking, she stopped and asked what I was looking at, so I told her, and shivers went up her spine. She told me, "I knew you were seeing something, because I looked at you and you had this expression on your face." And I did.

I was absolutely stunned by what I was seeing. I didn't even bother getting up to look for it outside, because I knew it wouldn't be there anymore. This was the first time I ever made my mom afraid, because she had to go outside right after that to let the dogs go to the bathroom.

Shortly after that, my mother said she saw something appear behind me. I was sitting on the couch next to the door of my father's office, and she said she saw a black cloud appear in the office doorway. She said it lingered there for a minute, but after a few seconds it slowly receded into the darkness of the office. Something surely was trying to get our attention that day.

My mother and I both witnessed the same figure outside on the porch one night. We were letting the dogs go to the bathroom before they got put to bed, and we both witnessed a thick white mist move across the backyard. My mother noticed it first as she saw it pass on the far end of the yard. When she mentioned this, I looked, and suddenly the mist blew right by me.

This was a cool encounter because both my mother and I witnessed it and could verify each other's experience, and there was nothing threatening about it. It was just a white mist. To me, it looked angelic. But I couldn't verify.

At that point, I asked my mom if she wanted to say hi to her dad (my grandfather/spirit guide).

She said, "Hey, Dad."

I took my headphones out and heard, "Hi there." This made her well-up with tears, knowing her dad was dead but not gone.

Things did not stop happening on the outside of the house. One afternoon in May of 2022, my father was sitting in the family room and he heard a noise. *Tap, tap, tap.* Three knocks on the window coming from the kitchen. This concerned me a little because, as previously described, the demonic always introduces itself in threes.

My dad said he got up to see if someone was in the backyard knocking on the windows, but he found nothing. The same thing started happening to my grandmother. She would tell me how she would hear three knocks on her door, and when she went...nobody was there. This was interesting to me.

I stopped giving these entities as much attention as I used to, and now they were redirecting their efforts to members of my family. I think this was their way of trying to get my attention, and make me worry. It didn't concern me that much, as long as nobody was being hurt (which nobody was). I mean yeah, I got scratched and raped at one point, but that kind of activity wasn't happening anymore. The family could deal with a few measly knocks and ghost sightings.

Things started moving around the house too. I went into the basement one day and one part of the sectional couch was moved apart from the others. At first, I thought that I had done this, but then I realized that I had even touched the part of the couch the night before.

Additionally, my mother witnessed something some people would be freaked out by—not us, though. She was sitting in my father's office watching YouTube videos when an item randomly got thrown from the top shelf of my father's bookcase onto the floor. My mom didn't give it too much thought; she just knew it was one of my "friends" trying to get some attention. She also heard a growl come from that room a few days prior to this happening, and it wasn't one of the dogs. She heard something growl at her and it puzzled her because she had no idea what to think about it. I personally think it was something trying to intimidate her, but the Koneys are not ones to be intimidated so easily.

We growl back.

I actually heard one of the growls myself, one day. I was using the restroom and it was dead quiet. All of a sudden, I heard this loud, extended growl. *Grrrrrrrrrr.* I thought it was my stomach for a second, then realized the sound came from in front of me rather than inside of me. I was even able to hear it through my headphones. Despite this entity's best attempts, this didn't scare me in the slightest. It was just a measly growl. I thought if they wanted to scare me then they'd have to do better than that.

One night, I actually got shoved by one of these entities. I was woken up from my sleep by the ominous feeling of an evil spirit around me. In my head, I said to the spirit, challenging it, "I bet you can't shove me." Then I felt my left shoulder get shoved causing me to roll halfway over. This was interesting to me. I fell right back asleep but reflected on it the next morning. *If they can push me at will, why don't they do that while I'm awake?* I think they need to wait until I'm asleep when my guard is down for them to make a move. This makes me wonder about how much paranormal activity/attacks I have slept through and haven't noticed. My guess is, probably a lot.

I also started seeing a lot of orbs around my house, specifically in the basement. So naturally, I took my phone out on several occasions and snapped some pictures. Below you will see some of the orbs, which are balls of spirit energy, that I captured in my basement. The orbs will be circled in blue so it's easier to locate them in the photos.

Orb number one was caught hovering next to the chandelier that hangs above our pool table.

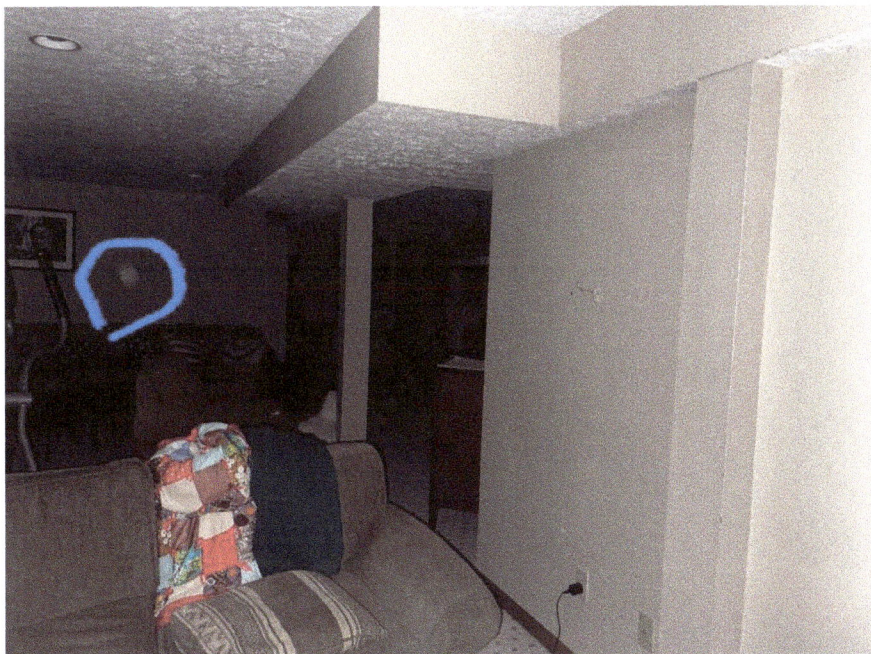

Orb number two was caught hovering just over my couch, about three feet in front of my face.

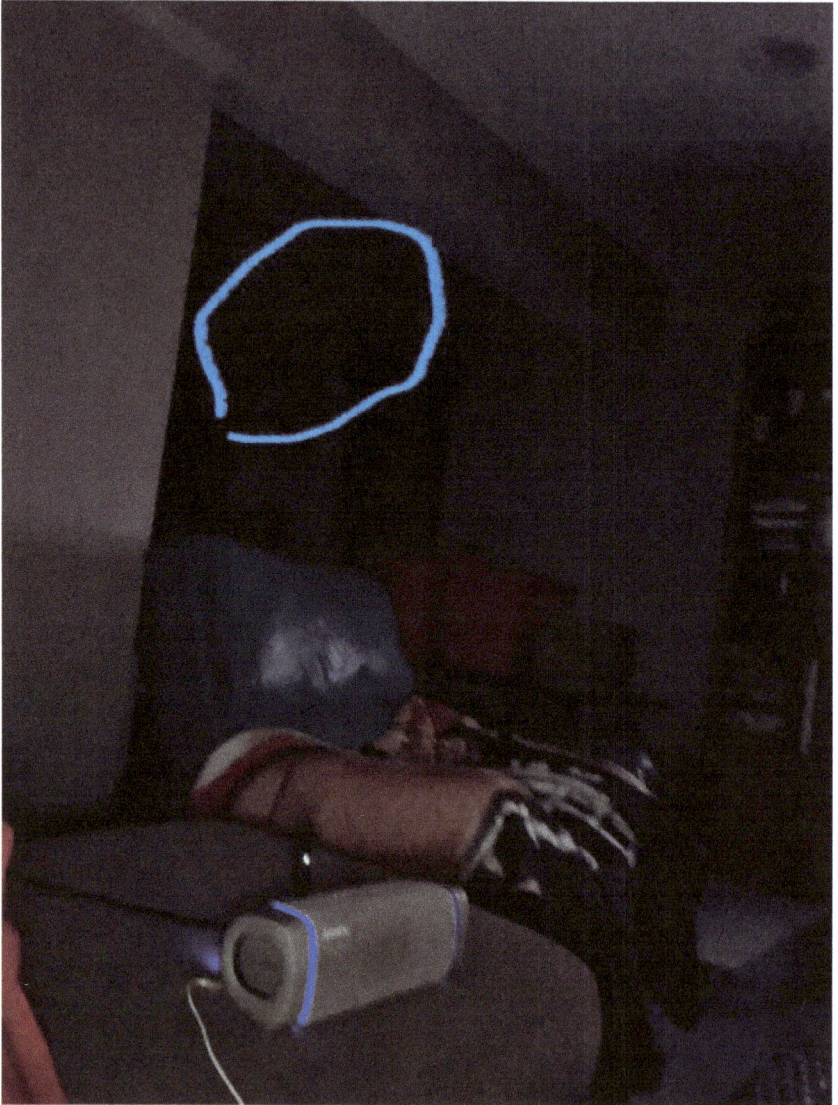

This next photo isn't an orb, but is an apparition. It is hard to see so again it is circled in blue. With a phone, it is easy to zoom in and see the figure, so if you can't see it, it is the bust of a person. Shoulders, head, eyes, face, and all. I would always see something standing in this area of the basement so I was thankful I was able to capture something on camera.

Orb number three was again caught near the pool table, this time flying by the lower woodwork of the table.

In Conclusion:
Where It Stands Today

Needless to say a lot has happened in the past year. It is June 9, 2022 as I write this, a year to the date that I had my abilities activated.

I have been through the spiritual gamut of paranormal experiences and back. To this day, I still see orbs (mostly black), I still see entities like the one that appeared in front of me last night as a shimmer of light and energy, I still deal with the voice of the unstable spirit telling me to kill myself, I still deal with the footsteps on the cushions when I'm sleeping, I still have to wear headphones wherever I go, and I still have a long way to go.

I have become a walking seance. I will continue to fight back, I will continue to piss them off (purely by existing and being me and enjoying life), and I will continue to come to terms with my abilities and vow to find a way to help people with them.

Maybe this book is helpful for a few. For those of you who made it through this book, thank you.

I hope I was able to shed some light on the spirit world and reveal how it can be both intoxicating and revolting, a blessing and toxic, a gift and a curse, all at the same time.

As far as dealing with the spirits still attached to me? I have begun to derive strength from their hatred. I've asked for help from God to help remove these spirits, and I haven't received a response yet. But I've learned that God's delay does not mean God's denial.

At the end of the day, I'm still here and I'm still standing, though on numb legs. My ultimate goal, you might wonder? I'm going to make them hate me because they can't break me! Sometimes, the sword has to free itself from the stone on its own.

I have experienced a plethora of bad things, but I believe the good will come. I'm not worried because I believe everything will come full circle. Thank you.

Author's Note

If you have experienced any supernatural or paranormal activity in your life, please feel free to email me at scott.g.koney@gmail.com for the consideration to be included in my next book.

I look forward to hearing from you.

ABOUT THE AUTHOR

Scott Koney is a Cleveland, Ohio native. With an interest in the paranormal his entire life, he would, at a very young age, become introduced to the world of the supernatural in ways he never thought possible. In his mid-twenties, Scott inhabited the gifts of being clairvisual and clairaudient (he can see and speak with the dead), but this was by no wish of his own. The gift he came to have was what inspired his writings, and his further interest in the supernatural.

www.ingramcontent.com/pod-product-compliance
Lightning Source LLC
Chambersburg PA
CBHW052116030426
42335CB00025B/3002